CREATED
—— *for* ——
GREATNESS

CREATED
— *for* —
GREATNESS

THE POWER *of*
MAGNANIMITY

Alexandre Havard

 Scepter

Copyright © 2014 by Scepter Publishers, Inc.
P.O. Box 1391
New Rochelle, NY 10801
www.scepterpublishers.org

All rights reserved.

Translation from the French by Anthony T. Salvia
Text and cover design by Rose Design

Printed in the United States of America

ISBN: 978-159417-217-5

ABOUT THE AUTHOR

Alexandre Havard is the author of the Virtuous Leadership system and the founder of the Havard Virtuous Leadership Institute (*www.hvli.org*). Born in Paris, he is a barrister by profession, having graduated from the René Descartes University, one of France's leading law schools, and practiced law in several European countries. He is now living and working in Moscow, where he offers seminars in Virtuous Leadership to senior business executives and university students. In the United States Alexandre Havard presented at the U.S. Army War College, the Harvard Business School and the Corporation Service Company (CSC). His book *Virtuous Leadership* (New York, Scepter Publishers, 2007) has been translated into fifteen languages.

In this depraved century—when European society is overcome with laziness, existential ennui and disbelief, when everywhere a bizarre mixture of hatred of life and fear of death reigns, when the best people sit idle, justifying their laziness and debauchery by their lack of clear life objectives—inspired souls are as necessary as the sun. These personalities are living evidence that in society there are still people of a higher order, people of heroic deeds, faith, and clearly defined objectives.

—Anton Pavlovich Chekhov

CONTENTS

3: Developing a Moral Sense

Conclusion   81

AUTHOR'S FOREWORD

In 1983, I took a break from my law studies in Paris to spend an unforgettable month with my Georgian great aunt, Elena, and her son Thamaz. They lived in Tbilisi, capital of the Soviet Republic of Georgia.

By the time I returned in 1990, the Soviet Union was on the verge of collapse and Aunt Elena had passed away. I was distressed to find that Thamaz had not yet fully recovered from his loss. He loved his mother more than anyone else. He had never left her side since the traumatic day in 1938 when his father was arrested and shot by the Communist secret police. He was then ten years old.

One evening, we drove to the cemetery to pay our respects to Aunt Elena. Thamaz was at the wheel of his Soviet-made Zhiguli. The closer we came to the cemetery, the more emotional Thamaz became. It had been raining. The road was bad. It was a slick, narrow mountain road, and it was nighttime. Suddenly, Thamaz turned towards me: "Are you afraid?" Ashamed to say otherwise, I replied, "No!" To my shock, he stepped on the accelerator.

I hardly had time to invoke my guardian angel when the car went sailing out over a precipice and down into the abyss, only to land some seconds later in the heart of the mountain cemetery. Its windshield shattered to bits, the

Zhiguli wound up suspended between two headstones. We had to exercise extreme caution in exiting the vehicle so as not to disturb the delicate balance. Several meters further on: a seemingly bottomless ravine.

We extricated ourselves gingerly and went down the mountain on foot and in silence without encountering a single vehicle. Thamaz finally said: "Too bad we ruined some headstones that didn't belong to us."

An hour later, we managed to flag down a car and hitched a ride back to Tbilisi. It was two o'clock in the morning.

For several days thereafter, I reflected on our misadventure. Although it ended badly, it could have been much worse. I was disappointed in Thamaz, but said nothing. Eventually, I understood that this sixty-year-old man had lost a long time ago—probably at the age of ten when his father was arrested by the Soviet KGB—not just a sense of orientation in life, but also a sense of life as such.

Often I think of Thamaz and of the millions of people wounded in one way or another by the ideological projects of the twentieth century. I think of the emptiness, the devastation it produced in hearts, and of current global policy, which, by focusing exclusively on economics, only aggravates these wounds.

I also think of all those who, unlike Thamaz, have known the warmth of hearth and home, because they had a father and a mother who loved them and educated them in truth, freedom, and virtue—and yet who, despite all of these advantages, for one reason or another, have not grasped the amplitude of their responsibilities before God and man, turn their backs on their vocation, or do not seek to discover and fulfill their mission in life.

It is to those men and women, whether young or not so young, that I dedicate this work.

INTRODUCTION

In *Virtuous Leadership: An Agenda for Personal Excellence*,[1] published in 2007 in the United States, I set forth my vision of leadership. This vision can be summarized in the following points:

1. *Authentic leadership must be based on an authentic anthropology, one that includes aretology, the science of virtues.* Virtue is a habit of the mind, the will and the heart, which allows us to achieve personal excellence and effectiveness. Leadership is intrinsically linked to virtue. First, because virtue creates trust—the *sine qua non* of leadership. Second, because virtue, which comes from the Latin *virtus*, meaning "strength" or "power," is a dynamic force that enhances the leader's capacity to act. Virtue allows the leader to do what people expect of him.

2. *Magnanimity and humility, which are principally virtues of the heart, constitute the essence of leadership.* Magnanimity is the habit of striving for great things. Leaders are magnanimous in their dreams, their visions, and their sense of mission; also in their capacity to challenge

---

1. A. Havard, *Virtuous Leadership: An Agenda for Personal Excellence* (New York: Scepter Publishers, 2007).

themselves and those around them. Humility is the habit of serving others. Humility means pulling rather than pushing, teaching rather than ordering about, inspiring rather than berating. Thus, leadership is less about displays of power than the empowerment of others. To practice humility is to bring out the greatness in others, to give them the capacity to realize their human potential. In this sense leaders are always teachers and fathers/mothers. Their "followers" are the ones they serve. Magnanimity and humility are virtues *specific* to leaders; together they constitute the *essence* of leadership.

3. *The virtues of prudence (practical wisdom), courage, self-control and justice, which are mainly virtues of the mind and the will, constitute the foundations of leadership.* Prudence increases the leader's ability to make right decisions; *courage* permits him to stay the course and resist pressures of all kinds; *self-control* subordinates his emotions and passions to the spirit and directs their vital energy to the fulfillment of the mission at hand; *justice* impels him to give everyone his due. If these four virtues, which are called cardinal, do not constitute the essence of leadership, they constitute its bedrock without which leadership comes to naught.

4. *Leaders are trained, not born.* Virtue is a habit acquired through practice. Leadership is a question of character (virtue, freedom, growth) and not of temperament (biology, conditioning, stagnation). Temperament can favor the growth of some virtues and

hinder the development of others. But there comes a point where the leader imposes his character on his temperament so much so that his temperament ceases to dominate him. Temperament is not an obstacle to leadership, whereas lack of character—i.e., the moral energy that prevents us from being slaves to biology—most definitely is.

5. *The leader does not lead by means of* potestas *or the power inherent in his office or functions. He leads by means of* auctoritas, *which proceeds from character.* Those who lead by means of *potestas*, because they lack authority, are leaders in name only. It is a vicious circle: he who lacks authority (*auctoritas*) tends to abuse his power (*potestas*), which provokes an erosion of authority, thus blocking his path towards authentic leadership. Leadership is not about rank or position or being on top of the heap. Leadership is a way of being, which can be lived by everyone no matter his or her place in society or in any given organization.

6. To grow in virtue, the heart, the will, and the mind come into play: we *contemplate* virtue through the heart, in order to perceive its intrinsic beauty and ardently desire it; we develop the habit of *acting* virtuously by means of the will; with the mind, we *practice* all the virtues simultaneously, paying particular attention to the virtue of prudence—the guide of all the virtues.

7. *By practicing the virtues, leaders become mature in their judgments, emotions, and behavior.* The signs of maturity

are self-confidence, coherence, psychological stability, joy, optimism, naturalness, freedom and responsibility, and interior peace. Leaders are neither skeptics nor cynics; they are realists. Realism is the capacity to entertain noble aspirations of the soul, despite one's personal weaknesses. Realists do not give in to weakness; they overcome it by the practice of virtues.

8. *Leaders reject a utilitarian approach to virtue.* Virtue is not something they cultivate in order to become effective at what they do. They cultivate virtue so as to realize themselves as human beings. We do not seek to grow in virtue in order to become more effective at what we do; improved effectiveness is merely one of virtue's many consequences.

9. *Leaders practice virtue ethics, rather than rules-based ethics.* Virtue ethics do not deny the validity of rules; they affirm that the essence of ethics is something other than rules. Rules must serve virtue. Virtue ethics underlie the leader's creativity, causing it to flourish.

10. *The practice of the specifically Christian virtues of faith, hope, and charity has a powerful impact on leadership.* These supernatural virtues elevate, reinforce, and transfigure the natural virtues of magnanimity and humility, which are the essence of leadership, and the natural virtues of prudence, courage, self-control, and justice, which constitute its foundations. No study of leadership would be complete that failed to take into account the supernatural virtues.

Created for Greatness represents a deepening of *Virtuous Leadership*. Together they constitute a unique and indivisible whole.

It required two years of concentrated research for me to understand that magnanimity and humility are the virtues specific to leaders. I arrived at this conclusion only after having studied the lives and behavior of a considerable number of leaders. Two years devoted to two words—that sounds pretty awful. Indeed, it would have been awful if it had been a question of two run-of-the-mill words. But magnanimity and humility are two words rich in meaning, possessed of extraordinary emotional and existential power, words that go straight to the heart because they embody a life ideal— the ideal of greatness and service.

I discovered that *leadership is a life ideal, because the specific virtues it draws on—magnanimity and humility— are themselves life ideals.* That discovery surprised and delighted me.

One can and should base one's *actions* on prudence, courage, self-control, and justice, but one can only base one's *existence* on magnanimity and humility, on the ideal of greatness and the ideal of service—in other words, on the ideal of leadership. *Magnanimity is the thirst to lead a full and intense life; humility is the thirst to love and sacrifice for others.* Consciously or unconsciously, the hearts of all human beings experience this thirst to live and to love. Magnanimity and humility are the *sine qua non* of personal fulfillment.

Magnanimity and humility are inextricably linked. They constitute a unique ideal: the ideal of the dignity and greatness of man. Magnanimity affirms our own personal dignity and greatness; humility affirms the dignity and greatness of others.

Magnanimity (i.e., greatness of heart), and humility are the fruits of a true appreciation of the value of man; pusillanimity (i.e., smallness of heart), which prevents man from understanding *himself*, and pride, which prevents him from understanding *others*, stem from a *false* appreciation of man's value. *Leadership is a life ideal that recognizes, assimilates, and propagates the truth about man.*

CHAPTER 1
The Ideal of Magnanimity

Magnanimity is an ideal rooted in trust in man, and his inherent greatness. It is the virtue of action. It is the supreme form of human hope. Magnanimity is a virtue capable of setting the tone of one's entire life, transforming it, giving it new meaning and leading to the flourishing of the personality. It is the first specific virtue of leaders.

I have been teaching students of widely differing cultures and languages and religions about magnanimity—this virtue specific to leadership—for ten years now. In my experience, magnanimity, everywhere and without fail, stirs the passions. I have seen people change fundamentally through their encounter with this virtue. And I have seen people flee from the lecture hall, as if terrorized by the very idea. Magnanimity leaves no one indifferent.

An affirmation of one's dignity and greatness

Aristotle was the first writer to elaborate a concept of magnanimity (*megalopsychia*). For him, the magnanimous person practices virtue, and, as a result, considers himself worthy of "great things" (by which he means honors). While the magnanimous person may well deserve honors, he does not seek them. He can do without them because he possesses something better—virtue, the greatest of treasures. He knows that the entire universe and everything in it is worth less than his virtue. He is aware of being worth more and of deserving better. But compared to the greatness of the virtue he possesses, all of that pales to insignificance.

Aristotle considered Socrates the model of the magnanimous person, although he never said so explicitly. Aristotelian magnanimity is that of the philosophers who hold the world in contempt the better to affirm man. It is equanimity in the face of the vicissitudes of life, indifference to dishonor (unless deserved), and contempt for the opinions of the multitude. It is not a question of pro-actively seeking to make things happen, but of putting up with things, of grinning and bearing it. Rather than developing one's abilities, the emphasis is on conquering oneself, on mastering one's autonomy and freedom. The magnanimous person affirms his human dignity and dominates a treacherous world, which he holds in contempt.

Aristotelian magnanimity affirms one's dignity and greatness. It is an exalted vision of self. This awareness of one's value is something we discover in all leaders. It is in fact the beginning of leadership. Without this awareness of one's dignity and greatness there is no magnanimity and no leadership.

Take the case of General de Gaulle. He refused to accept France's capitulation to Germany in 1940. Although a mere brigadier general and completely unknown to his countrymen, he was determined to vindicate France's honor by calling the nation to resistance, which he would do in his famous address to the French nation over the airwaves of the BBC on June 18, 1940. But that was yet to come. His vision of the task at hand was preceded by his unshakable faith in his own dignity and greatness. This comes through in his *War Memoirs*: "Limited and alone though I was, and precisely because I was so, I had to ascend to the heights, never then to come down."[1]

Abraham Lincoln had such an exalted vision of self that to become the President of the United States was for him "the most natural thing to do." *New York Times* Editor Henry Raymond observed:

> Nothing was more marked in Mr. Lincoln's personal demeanor than its utter unconsciousness of his position. It would be difficult, if not impossible, to find another man who would not, upon a sudden transfer from the obscurity of private life in a country town to the dignities and duties of the Presidency, feel it incumbent upon him to assume something of the manner and tone befitting that position. Mr. Lincoln never seemed to be aware that

---

1. C. de Gaulle, *The Complete War Memoirs of Charles de Gaulle* (New York: Carroll & Graf Publishers, 1998), 82.

his place or his business were essentially different from those in which he had always been engaged.[2]

Leadership begins with an exalted vision of self. Only then does it acquire a vision of what it seeks to achieve.

When Darwin Smith became CEO of Kimberly-Clark in 1971, his company had a secure position in its sector. But Smith believed that he and his company were capable of much more. His exalted vision of self allowed him to set the objective: to achieve greatness or perish. He decided to sell all of its factories that had been producing coated paper—the main source of the company's revenue—and used the proceeds to begin producing consumer paper products, deliberately placing the firm in direct competition with market leaders Procter & Gamble and Scott Paper.[3] This decision brought about a spectacular turnaround in the firm's fortunes: it transformed Kimberly-Clark into the number one paper-based consumer-products company in the world.

Smith's sense of personal worth and dignity instilled in him an ill-disguised contempt for the opinions of the multitude. Wall Street analysts and the business media derided his decision; they were certain it would fail. Smith, like Socrates, did not consult the mob for its opinion.

---

2. Henry Raymond, *The Life, Public Services, and State Papers of Abraham Lincoln*, Volume II, 723–724.

3. About D. Smith, cf. A. Havard, *Virtuous Leadership*, part 1, chapter 1.

The virtue of action

For Thomas Aquinas, the most important philosopher and theologian of the Middle Ages, magnanimity is the insatiable appetite for great things (*extensio animi ad magna);* the magnanimous person is one whose heart is set on conquering the world and achieving personal excellence.

Magnanimity is a longing for greatness—a burning desire, a sacred quest, an aspiration. *Magnanimitas,* the Latin word coined by Cicero in 44 BC to render the Greek *megalopsychia,* is equivalent to *magnitudo animi,* observes Aquinas, and *animus* implies irascible power, the instinct for combat and conquest. Magnanimity is the virtue of aggressiveness; it is ever prepared to attack, to conquer, to act with the impetuosity of a lion.

In 1963 Martin Luther King wrote from his prison cell:

> My Dear Fellow Clergymen: While confined here in the Birmingham city jail, I came across your recent statement calling my present activities 'unwise and untimely. . . . For years now I have heard the word "Wait!" It rings in the ear of every Negro with piercing familiarity. This "Wait" has almost always meant "Never." . . . I have almost reached the regrettable conclusion that the Negro's great stumbling block in his stride toward freedom is not the White Citizen's Counciler or the Ku Klux Klanner, but the white moderate . . . , who paternalistically believes he can set the timetable for another man's

freedom; who lives by a mythical concept of time and who constantly advises the Negro to wait for a "more convenient season" . . . We have waited for more than 340 years for our constitutional and God given rights. . . . I have just received a letter from a white brother in Texas. He writes: "All Christians know that the colored people will receive equal rights eventually, but it is possible that you are in too great a religious hurry. It has taken Christianity almost two thousand years to accomplish what it has. The teachings of Christ take time to come to earth." Such an attitude stems from a tragic misconception of time, from the strangely irrational notion that there is something in the very flow of time that will inevitably cure all ills. . . .

More and more I feel that the people of ill will have used time much more effectively than have the people of good will. We will have to repent in this generation not merely for the hateful words and actions of the bad people but for the appalling silence of the good people. Human progress never rolls in on wheels of inevitability; it comes through the tireless efforts of men willing to be coworkers with God, and without this hard work, time itself becomes an ally of the forces of social stagnation. We must use time creatively, in the knowledge that the time is always ripe to do right.

King "recognized the urgency of the moment." A few months later he organized and led the

Million Man March and delivered his historic "I Have a Dream" speech in which he called for an end to racism. Although introspective, and, indeed, melancholic by nature, King took direct action out of his boundless magnanimity.

Aquinas takes up the formulae of Aristotle, but gives them a different meaning. Whereas Aristotle says the magnanimous man considers himself worthy of great things (great honors), Aquinas says he considers himself worthy of *doing* great things, which he aims to accomplish for themselves and their inherent grandeur. At the same time, he finds that, without wanting to, he has merited honor, and now must make good use of it.

Aristotle affirms man's greatness in declaring his autonomy from the world because he fears the fates are intent on crushing him. Aquinas, however, affirms man's greatness in conquering the world because he believes it is the work of God, and is, therefore, good.

Magnanimity is the conquest of greatness. It is not content to initiate; it achieves. It is not content to aspire to greatness, but to attain it. It is like jet fuel: it is the propulsive virtue *par excellence*. Magnanimity is the virtue of action; there is more energy in it than in mere audacity. The magnanimous person achieves self-fulfillment in and through action. He gives himself over to it with passion and enthusiasm.

For the true leader, action always stems from self-awareness. It is never mere *activism*, and never degenerates into *workaholism*. Leaders are always *doers*, but never do things just for the sake of doing them; their doing is always an extension of their being, the outgrowth of their contemplation of their own dignity and greatness. Non-leaders act merely in order to achieve established objectives, and, often, to escape themselves, and somehow fill the emptiness of their interior lives.

Personal excellence is the ultimate aim of magnanimity: The most ambitious project is misguided if it does not foster at the same time the development of the virtue, character, and personal excellence of all those involved in it.

For leaders, the achievement of important organizational goals is never an end in itself, but only a means to the higher end of growth for all concerned. If Darwin Smith took great risks, it was because he knew that the personal growth generated by acting outstrips the potential material results, no matter how brilliant or lucrative. To get things done is management; to make people grow is leadership. Smith was an outstanding manager, but he was above all a magnificent leader. He cared more for people than for things. He was fully aware that personal excellence—his own, and that of the people he led— is a greater good than material success.

The supreme form of human hope

Action is the result of hope. The stronger the hope, the more exalted the goal. Magnanimity stimulates hope, rendering it engaging, exalting, intoxicating.

In June 1940, utterly alone and in exile in England, General de Gaulle gave the world a powerful lesson in hope. "I seemed to myself, alone as I was and deprived of everything, like a man on the shore of an ocean, proposing to swim across."[4] Nevertheless, objective difficulties did not stop him; he threw himself into action, never doubting his ability to rally the French nation to resistance and lead it to victory.

Hope sees beyond all obstacles; it strives for the great good regardless of objective difficulties. Inspired by the task at hand—at once noble and arduous—the heart and soul are engaged to the full.

Eric Liddell, winner of the gold medal in the 400-metres race at the 1924 Olympic Games, and one of the runners portrayed in the popular film *Chariots of Fire*, was once knocked to the ground by a competitor at the very outset of a race. By the time he got back on his feet, he found himself 20 meters behind the pack. Nevertheless, he hurled himself forward, caught up with the others and surpassed them just before the finish line. Crossing the tape ahead of the pack, he crumpled to the ground, exhausted and triumphant.

Hope is a joyful enthusiasm. It is a taste for the effort involved, the joy of the search, which already, in a certain way, contains within it the good to which it aspires. Eric Liddell, a man of strong religious faith, expressed something of the adventurous quality of hope when he said, "When I run, I feel His pleasure."

---

4. C. de Gaulle, op. cit., 81.

Magnanimity—*human* hope—is an ideal imbued with trust in man. It must not be confused with theological hope, which is about trust in God; in the words of Saint Paul: "I can do all things in him who strengthens me."[5]

Magnanimity is a *natural* virtue which man can acquire and develop through his own efforts; *supernatural* hope is a virtue infused by God in the soul, and which, along with faith and charity, is one of the three theological virtues.

Christian theologians of the Middle Ages did not make this distinction. What they called magnanimity was actually the supernatural virtue of hope. For them, one was magnanimous if one was conscious of one's own misery, and sought in God alone the power to overcome the world.[6]

It is Thomas Aquinas in the thirteenth century who, after having read a faithful translation of Aristotle's works, restored magnanimity's true meaning. For him, as for Aristotle, magnanimity is an ideal of the greatness of *man*, an ideal of trust in *man*. Aquinas clearly differentiates the natural virtue of magnanimity from the supernatural virtue of hope.

Aquinas' restoration of the human is one of the great achievements in the history of Christian thought. Christian humanism, in all of its amplitude, is born of it.

---

5. Philippians 4:13.

6. Cf. R. A. Gauthier, *Magnanimité: l'idéal de grandeur dans la philosophie païenne et dans la théologie chrétienne* (Paris: Vrin, 1951).

The magnanimous Christian expects everything of himself as if God did not exist (magnanimity), and expects everything of God as if he could do nothing on his own (theological hope). He behaves like an adult on the natural plane, and like a child on the supernatural one. But this supernatural childhood is not passive: supernatural hope, like human hope, does not shy away from difficulty; on the contrary, it arouses the soul, directing it to the conquest of the good. There is only one psychology of hope.

Magnanimity and theological hope complement each other perfectly in the leader who lives his Christian faith. Consider the case of Aleksandr Solzhenitsyn, the Russian writer and recipient of the Nobel Prize for literature,[7] whose natural hope was reinforced by his theological hope. He resisted several decades of persecution by a totalitarian regime sworn to his destruction, devoting all of his life and work to commemorating the many millions of human beings who were done to death by the Communist system. Here is a prayer he composed in times of hardship:

How easy it is to live with you, Lord!
How easy to believe in you!
When my mind casts about
Or flags in bewilderment,
When the cleverest among us

---

7. About A. Solzhenitsyn, cf. A. Havard, *Virtuous Leadership*, part 1, chapter 1.

Cannot see past the present evening,

Not knowing what to do tomorrow,

You send me the clarity to know

That you exist

And will take care

That not all of the paths of goodness should be barred.[8]

Solzhenitsyn's life shows that magnanimity and theological hope can coexist harmoniously in the leader who practices his Christian faith. This great leader trusted fully both in himself and in God. He trusted in his own capacity for action and in God's help.

The day before his assassination, on April 3, 1968, Martin Luther King, a man full of human, natural hope, revealed in his famous "I've Been to the Mountaintop" oration the relevance for him personally, as a Baptist minister, of *supernatural* hope:

> Like anybody, I would like to live a long life; longevity has its place. But I'm not concerned about that now. I just want to do God's will. And He's allowed me to go up to the mountain. And I've looked over. And I've seen the Promised Land. I may not get there with you. But I want you to know tonight, that we, as a people, will get to the Promised Land. So I'm happy, tonight. I'm not worried

8. A. Solzhenitsyn, *Krokhotki* (1958–1963) (Moskva: EKSMO, 2010).

about anything. I'm not fearing any man. Mine eyes
have seen the glory of the coming of the Lord.

King's natural hope was clearly reinforced by his
supernatural hope.

Magnanimity and humility go hand in hand

As we noted in the Introduction, humility is the habit
of service. But there is more to humility than that; it is
also the awareness that man is fully dependent on God,
his Creator. We call this aspect of the virtue "metaphysical humility" in order to differentiate it from
"fraternal humility," which is the habit of service.

In speaking of magnanimity, we need to consider
"metaphysical humility." The more aware we become
of our personal greatness, the more we need to understand that greatness is a gift of God. Magnanimity
without humility is no magnanimity at all. It is self-
betrayal and can easily lead to personal calamities of
one kind or another.

Magnanimity and humility go hand in hand: In
specifically human endeavors, man has the right and
the duty to trust in himself (this is magnanimity), without losing sight of the fact that the human capacities on
which he relies come from God (this is humility). The
magnanimous impulse to embark on great endeavors
should always be joined to the detachment that stems
from humility, which allows one to perceive God in all
things. Man's exaltation must always be accompanied
by abasement before God. "When I was struggling

against the Communist regime," Solzhenitsyn wrote, "I understood that it was not I who was fighting, that I am an insect, that in carrying on such a struggle I was just a tool in the hands of Another."[9] Because he was truly magnanimous, Solzhenitsyn understood himself to be a (powerful) tool in the hands of God; and because he was truly humble, he openly acknowledged that he was *only* a tool.

He who is magnanimous and humble *magnanimously* assesses his talents and abilities and judges himself worthy of great things, which he undertakes with confidence; at the same time, he *humbly* perceives his status as a creature and understands that his capacities and his virtues, even those acquired by his personal efforts, are ultimately gifts of God. This fills him with gratitude to God and can only increase the strength of his hope.

Humility acknowledges the strength and greatness of man, seeing them as gifts of God. It constitutes no denial of man's own greatness and strength to humbly attribute them to the goodness of God. Humility offers up to God this greatness and strength, thereby consecrating them.

Many Christians believe in God, but few believe in themselves, in their talents and capabilities. As their concept of humility excludes magnanimity, such people cannot—and will not—lead. It comes as no surprise,

---

9. Ogoniok, 1998/4559/24-52-53.

then, that the Western world today rarely recruits its political leaders among believing Christians.

The most influential leaders of the past three hundred years were not Christians. This is not because Christians were expelled from social life; it is because so many Christians voluntarily withdrew from it. It is the most astonishing case of the self-castration of a whole community in the history of humanity.

Christians should reflect on Joan of Arc, nowadays so much despised in France, her homeland, and so beloved in England, the land of her enemy. Joan was a true Christian; she was truly magnanimous. In the words of G.K. Chesterton, "Joan of Arc was not stuck at the cross-roads, either by rejecting all the paths like Tolstoy or by accepting them all like Nietzsche. She chose a path, and went down it like a thunderbolt. . . . Tolstoy only praised the peasant; she was the peasant. Nietzsche only praised the warrior; she was the warrior. She beat them both at their own antagonistic ideals; she was more gentle than the one, more violent than the other."[10]

Joan became the supreme commander of French military forces at the age of seventeen. Her mission was to assure the coronation of the crown prince, and, while she was at it, expel the English from France. She had an exalted vision of herself and her mission. She used to say with deep satisfaction: "It was for this that

---

10. G.K. Chesterton, *The Suicide of Thought in Orthodoxy*, chapter III.

I was born!" Leonard Cohen, the Canadian poet and singer, captured something of her greatness when he wrote his "Joan of Arc," a dialogue between Joan and the fire consuming her at the stake as English soldiers look on:

> I love your solitude, I love your pride
>
> . . .
>
> I saw her wince, I saw her cry,
> I saw the glory in her eye.[11]

Joan famously said: "Help yourself and God will help you." She trusted fully in God, and fully in herself. When asked why she needed an army if God wished to deliver the French people, she answered: "The soldiers will fight and He will grant victory."

"Joan of Arc was a being so uplifted from the ordinary run of mankind," affirms Winston Churchill, "that she finds no equal in a thousand years."[12]

Modern society needs men and women who believe in *man*. Saint Paul, the apostle of theological hope, is also the apostle of the *humanity* of Christ: he saw in Jesus Christ the *perfect Man*,[13] the man who practiced all of the *human* virtues to perfection, including magnanimity. Saint Paul was probably the most magnanimous of the apostles. He practiced human hope—not

---

11. L. Cohen, *Songs of Love and Hate*, "Joan of Arc," 1971.

12. W. Churchill, *The Birth of Britain*, chapter 26.

13. Cf. Ephesians 4:13.

only theological hope—to the full. His human energy reinforced by God's grace made him probably the greatest Christian *doer* of all times.

A Christian must certainly be aware of his human shortcomings and seek in God the strength to overcome the world. But this is not sufficient. He must also be aware of his own talents, and learn to rely on them and have recourse to all human means. This is a vital pre-condition for leadership.

Purify your intentions

Vanity is the search for a false greatness. It is the quest for one's own honor and glory. To be known and honored does not contribute to the perfection of man. Greatness is to be found elsewhere—in virtue and in the attainment of human excellence.

There is nothing inherently wrong with honor and glory, but the magnanimous person never seeks them for their own sake. To crave them is to jeopardize the attainment of virtue.

Vanity sets in when glory and honor become motives to act, even if only secondary ones. Nothing we do is totally bad if, in doing it, we seek virtue for itself, for its own beauty, and seek honor and glory only secondarily. The action remains in itself virtuous, but a good motive is mixed with a bad one: the good and the bad mingle. It requires a lot of work over an extended period of time to destroy this subtle form of vanity and achieve perfect purity of intention.

Magnanimity is not megalomania

A student once asked me: "Vladimir Lenin, Adolf Hitler, and Margaret Sanger[14] were evil, but, in the end, weren't they magnanimous?"

In order to be magnanimous, first you need to possess the virtue of prudence, or, practical wisdom. Prudence is the guiding light of all the virtues, because it reveals how to behave virtuously in any situation. If you are not prudent, you will not be able to distinguish megalomaniacal behavior from magnanimous behavior.

Lenin, Hitler, and Sanger practiced cunning, not prudence; megalomania, not magnanimity. They had no interest in prudence, because they had no interest in goodness.

Some writers say Lenin, Hitler, and Sanger exhibited value-free leadership; in fact what they exhibited was not leadership at all, but manipulation, and of a decidedly satanic kind. Leadership can only be virtuous or it is not leadership. The Ancient Greeks understood this perfectly.[15] So do modern people who have not taken leave of their senses.

Magnanimity and self-esteem are two different things

Do not confuse magnanimity with self-esteem. Magnanimity is a virtue, self-esteem a mere feeling (which

---

14. About M. Sanger, cf. A. Havard, *Virtuous Leadership*, part 1, chapter 3.

15. Read, for instance, the *Agesilaus* of Xenophon (444–354 BC).

is not to say it is not a good thing). A virtue is something stable and objective; feelings tend to be unstable, and are always subjective. You may wake up in the morning with a huge amount of self-esteem, and go to bed that night feeling lousy about yourself.

Magnanimity is something you are; self-esteem is something you have. One may be small of heart and at the same time possess enormous self-esteem. The opposite is also true: a magnanimous person may have very little self-esteem.

Just because you feel great about yourself does not mean you have attained personal greatness, or that you are aware of your gifts and talents. All you need to feel great about yourself is flattery. Whereas magnanimity stems from self-knowledge, self-esteem depends on how others see us.

The "virtue of youth"

Young people are usually better able to practice magnanimity than the elderly. That is because young people tend to be hopeful about the future and to dream of accomplishing great things. Older people, not surprisingly, tend to dwell on the past and be more concerned to secure life's necessities than to blaze new trails.[16]

But the reality is sometimes more complex. Magnanimity need not be a question of age. There are lazy young devoid of ambition, and magnanimous older

---

16. Cf. Aristotle, *Rhétoric*, II, 12, 1389 a 18–32 and 1389 b 25–27.

people driven to accomplish great things. In other words, there are young people who are effectively "old" and old people who are really quite "young." Despite having spent sixteen years in Soviet prisons and concentration camps, the Russian engineer and writer Dmitri Panin would remain youthful, possessed of a generous soul, and filled with hope and optimism, even until his death in 1987 in exile in France. In the late 1940s, Panin served in the same Gulag camp as Aleksandr Solzhenitsyn, who depicted him as Dmitri Sologdin in his classic novel, *In the First Circle*:

> Dmitri Sologdin . . . was a non-entity, a slave without rights. He had been inside for twelve years, but because he had been sentenced to a second term, there was no knowing when, if ever, his imprisonment would end. His wife had wasted her youth waiting in vain for him. To avoid dismissal from her present job, as from so many others, she had pretended that she had no husband and had stopped writing to him. Sologdin had never seen his only son—his wife had been pregnant when he was arrested. Sologdin had gone through the forests of Cherdynsk [ed., in the northern Urals], the mines of Vorkuta [ed., above the Arctic Circle], two periods under investigation, one of six months, one of a year, tormented by lack of sleep, drained of his strength, wasting away. His name and his future had long ago been trampled into the mud. All he possessed was a pair of well-worn padded trousers and

a tarpaulin work jacket, kept at present in the store-room in expectation of worse times to come. He was paid thirty rubles a month—enough for three kilos of sugar—but not in cash. He could breathe fresh air only at stated times authorized by the prison authorities.

And in his soul there was a peace that nothing could destroy. His eyes sparkled like those of a young man. His chest, bared to the frost, heaved as though he were experiencing life to the full.[17]

The soul, the eyes, the chest—peace, light, and fullness of life . . . Few writers since Aristotle have captured the *corporal* dimension of magnanimity with such precision and economy of means.

When we say that magnanimity is the virtue of youth, we do not mean that young people are magnanimous; we mean that magnanimous people remain young in spirit no matter their age.

Nevertheless, magnanimous people who are actually young in years are something special: they are a gift to humanity. They impress us. They constantly remind us of what is important, and what is not. They shake us out of our routine and inspire us to live life to the full.

In his poem "The Fool," Padraic Pearse, the Anglo-Irish barrister, poet, and a leader of Irish Republican

17. A. Solzhenitsyn, *In the First Circle* (New York: Harper Perennial, 2009), 171.

forces in the Easter Rebellion of 1916 (only to be executed for his part in the Rising), expressed with great intensity the radicalism of magnanimity, which is proper to youth:

> I have squandered the splendid years that the Lord God gave to my youth
>
> In attempting impossible things, deeming them alone worth the toil.
>
> Was it folly or grace? Not men shall judge me, but God.
>
> I have squandered the splendid years:
>
> Lord, if I had the years I would squander them over again. . . .
>
> Yea, ere my hot youth pass, I speak to my people and say:
>
> Ye shall be foolish as I; ye shall scatter, not save;
>
> Ye shall venture your all, lest ye lose what is more than all . . .

It was after a few encounters with university students that I gave up my career as a lawyer and dedicated myself to studying and teaching leadership. I was lecturing on the history of European integration and spent hours helping young people enter the hearts and minds of the European Union's Founding Fathers: Robert Schuman, Konrad Adenauer, Alcide de Gasperi, Jean Monnet. My students were amazed by their greatness; I found their enthusiasm infectious and uplifting.

Young people in their magnanimity brought me to leadership, and if someday I quit teaching business executives, I will never quit teaching young people: one needs to inhale before exhaling; likewise, I need to witness hope before speaking about it.

A virtue capable of embracing all of life

According to Plato, the principal human virtues are prudence, justice, courage, and self-control. Ambrose of Milan called them *the cardinal virtues* because all the other virtues depend on them. The word cardinal derives from the Latin *cardo*, which means hinge. Just as a door hangs on a hinge, so all of the virtues hang on the cardinal ones. Every act of virtue requires 1) prudence, which allows us to discern the good in every situation; 2) justice, which impels us to achieve it; 3) courage, which gives us strength, endurance, and perseverance in achieving it; and 4) self-control, which keeps the passions from leading us to the opposite of the good.

The cardinal virtues are the "basic virtues," which does not mean they are the greatest of the virtues. Aristotle called magnanimity the "ornament of the virtues" because it allows the other virtues to achieve perfection. In this sense, it is superior to the cardinal virtues.

Magnanimity inspires a new vigor and a new passion in the practice of the other virtues, drawing them into its quest for greatness, impelling them to surpass themselves.

What the magnanimous person seeks in each virtue is not only the good specific to it, but also the greatness contained within it, the flourishing of his personality and the perfection he achieves through it. By the same token, what the magnanimous person flees in fleeing vice is not the evil specific to it, but rather the smallness, the diminution in stature, the decline implicit in it.

Magnanimity defines a lifestyle centered on the flourishing of the human personality.

CHAPTER 2

The Ideal of Humility

Humility is the second virtue specific to leaders. Whereas magnanimity affirms our personal dignity and greatness, humility affirms the dignity and greatness of others. Leadership means pulling rather than pushing, teaching rather than ordering about, inspiring rather than berating. Thus, leadership is less about displays of power than the empowerment of others. To practice humility is to bring out the greatness in others, to give them the capacity to realize their human potential. In this sense, leaders are always teachers and fathers/mothers. Humility is the habit of serving others. A leader's "followers" are the people he serves.

No less than magnanimity, humility inflames the souls of generous people even as it strikes terror in the hearts of egoists. And yet it is easier to talk to people about magnanimity than humility: many want to be great; few want to hear about service. *The fact is, one cannot become great if one is not prepared to serve others. It is precisely in serving others that one becomes great.*

John Wooden, one of America's most revered basketball coaches (he won ten national championships in a 12-year period), used to say: "Personal greatness for any leader is measured by effectiveness in bringing out the greatness in those you lead."[1]

If magnanimity energizes the flourishing of the personality, humility gives direction to this energy.

Becoming great by bringing out the greatness in others

Leadership is not an exercise in individualism. Magnanimity excludes egoism, which impels us to deny the importance of others even as we revel in our own.

"The lie and evil of egoism does not consist in the egoist having too high an opinion of himself, or believing himself to be of boundless importance and infinite dignity," says Russian philosopher Vladimir Soloviev. "He is right about that . . . Every person possesses absolute meaning and dignity and cannot value himself too highly. . . . The fundamental lie and evil of egoism is not in this absolute self-consciousness and self-regard of the subject, but rather, having ascribed to himself by right an unconditional importance, in unfairly denying the importance of others; recognizing himself as the center of life, which in fact he is, he relegates others to the

---

1. J. Wooden and S. Jamison, *Wooden on Leadership* (New York: McGraw-Hill, 2007), 179.

margins of existence, attributing to them only a superficial and relative value."[2]

In acknowledging our own dignity and greatness, we must also acknowledge the dignity and greatness of others, and serve them. Through his *humble* magnanimity (a magnanimity directed towards service), Darwin Smith brought out the greatness in his colleagues. Similarly, Joan of Arc, through her *humble* magnanimity, brought out the greatness in her soldiers and changed the hearts of millions of her countrymen. Seven years after her death, just as she had predicted, the English were driven from French soil. This event was of minor importance compared to the spiritual revival of France that Joan engendered.

The example of Michelin

When François Michelin took over as head of the Michelin tire company in 1954, he was 28 years old. He has occupied the office of Edouard Michelin, his grandfather and founder of the company, ever since. It is a small space notable for its modesty. One day, an employee who was about to retire called on François to say goodbye. The employee recalled that when he was sixteen years old his job was to distribute mail throughout the company. One day, he was asked to personally deliver a letter to François's grandfather, Edouard. The 16-year-old knocked on the door of his

---

2. V. Soloviev, *The Meaning of Love*, 2-III.

office; Edouard's voice came through the door: "Please come in, *monsieur* [trans., sir], and have a seat." This sign of respect on the boss's part made a big impact on the young employee. Edouard's words and demeanor remained in the employee's heart from that day on. The founder of the company showed deep respect for other people, no matter their station in life.

François Michelin is heir to this tradition. He is aware that "monsieur" is a contraction of "mon seigneur" [trans., my Lord]. It means recognizing this unique human being who possesses a part of the truth that I do not possess.

When François Michelin speaks, his language is simple, accessible to all, a language that workers, trade unionists and managers understand: "If I use simple words when I speak, it's simply to be sure *I* understand what I am saying." This is no mere self-deprecating quip, but a reflection of his profound respect for the people he is addressing.

In January 2010, I visited François Michelin at his company's headquarters in Clermont-Ferrand, central France. Our interview lasted two and a half hours, during which he took three important telephone calls. These calls, as I learned later, concerned a campaign of calumny being waged against him in the media. This must have been very unpleasant for him, and yet François did not seem in the least perturbed or distracted. He was completely absorbed in our conversation. He would return smiling, apologize, look me straight in the eye, and pick up the conversation where we left off. In François Michelin one observes self-mastery, serenity, and, above all, respect for other people, for each unique and irreplaceable person, and a great desire to serve.

"What strikes me about François Michelin," says Carlos Ghosn, CEO of Renault, "it's the attention he pays to people, his concern to foster the growth of the people around him. He has great ambition for his firm, an ambition that is not destructive of those who are there to help him achieve it. . . . His interior self is even stronger than his captain-of-industry self."[3]

To serve others, first you have to know how to listen to them. "Look at my ears," François Michelin said. "They're distended. It's the diploma I value most."

For François Michelin to help a person become what he is, this is what counts above all. It was this spirit that allowed Marius Mignol, a worker without formal education, to invent the radial tire that revolutionized the industry. When he was hired, Mignol was supposed to work in the company's print shop, but Edouard Michelin told the firm's head of personnel: "Don't judge by appearances. Remember that one must break the stone to find the diamond hidden inside."

Mignol was re-assigned to a purely commercial part of the business involving international markets. One day, Edouard Michelin noticed a strange slide ruler on his desk. It was a device Mignol had invented

---

3. "Michelin—Son histoire, ses champions, les héros du quotidien," La Montagne, numéro hors série (Nov. 2007).

to rapidly convert foreign exchange rates. Edouard was impressed by the ingenuity of the thing. He understood that Mignol was a genius. Soon, the firm transferred Mignol to the research division at a critical time for the industry. The conventional tire of that time had reached the limits of its usefulness because of its tendency to heat up at high speeds. To study variations in heat inside the conventional tire, Mignol invented a *"cage à mouche,"* or "fly trap," a tire whose sides were replaced by metallic cables with plenty of space between them. The resulting "radial tire" proved revolutionary.

It was because Edouard Michelin was interested in people and their personal and professional growth that Marius Mignol was able to discover his talents and put them at the service of others.

François Michelin's respect for people and desire to serve is a manifestation of his humility, but it is also a matter of good sense. "It is often said that facts are stubborn, but in reality it is we who are stubborn," he says. "We refuse to accept facts; we refuse to accept the truth about man. We fixate on things, whereas the most powerful engine of enterprise is *human* energy."

Humility, far from being an obstacle to the growth and development of an enterprise, is critically important to its success: the Michelin tire company has grown to be the world's number 1 firm in its sector.

Humility as an ideal

The ideal of fraternal humility—i.e., service—took root in the Greco-Latin world not through antique philosophy, but through Christianity. As Jesus Christ said, "For the Son of man also came not to be served but to serve . . . I am among you as one who serves."[4] Christ summarized humility in his commandment that we serve one another: "Whoever would be great among you must be your servant."[5]

To understand the meaning of humility, it is first necessary to understand who God is, because God, in himself, is a family and each member of this family is a perfect model of humility. The three divine Persons—the Father, the Son and the Holy Spirit—commune among themselves in a manner so complete that each exists only for the others. In God, to be a Person means being a "gift" for the others. By the same token, for man to be a person means being a "gift" for others. Without this humility it is impossible to realize oneself as a person.[6]

We serve people when we meet their needs, material and spiritual. And the most exalted way to serve is to bring out the greatness in others. Christ served his disciples by constantly teaching them, correcting them, and challenging them. Christ served his disciples by bringing out their personal greatness.

---

4. Mark 10:45 (Matthew 20:28) and Luke 22:27.

5. Matthew 20:26.

6. Cf. St. John Paul II, Apostolic Letter, *Mulieris Dignitatem* (*On the Dignity and Vocation of Women*) August 15, 1988, 7.

Fraternal humility is one of the fruits of authentic love. You love people above all when you help them grow as human beings, as persons, as children of God; when you help them fulfill God's command to "be perfect, as your heavenly Father is perfect."[7] Perfection, excellence, holiness—these are synonyms for greatness.

Humility, like magnanimity, is a source of joy. In serving others with his heart, mind and will, the leader discovers the meaning and the value of his life; he experiences the greatness of human dignity and the mystical link that unites all of humanity. Pride and egoism, like pusillanimity, are sources of sadness, bitterness, and pessimism.

---

7. Matthew 5:48.

CHAPTER 3

Developing a Moral Sense

We have pointed out some key aspects of magnanimity and humility—the virtues specific to leaders. It remains to consider how leaders can develop these virtues, which is the whole point of life, and of this book. But before we get to that point, it behooves us to take a look at how we develop the moral sense that is the pre-condition for growing in virtue.

Listen to your conscience and obey it faithfully

To develop a moral sense, above all, one needs to listen to one's conscience and live accordingly.

Vera Gangart, the fictitious heroine of Aleksandr Solzhenitsyn's *Cancer Ward*, died in the spring of 2007 and was laid to rest in Helsinki, Finland. Actually, it was Dr. Irina Meyke who passed away, for it was she who served as the basis for Solzhenitsyn's literary invention. I met Irina just several months before she died and she told me her remarkable story.

Irina was serving as an oncologist in Tashkent, capital of the Uzbek Soviet Socialist Republic, when, in January of 1954, she first laid eyes on Solzhenitsyn. He was then a 35-year-old Red Army officer and aspiring writer, who, having endured years in Soviet labor camps and prisons, was now suffering from abdominal cancer. "No one could have survived both the camps and cancer. But he could. I had to help him; he had to live!"

Irina devoted all of her professional skill and energies to curing this survivor of the Gulag, this "enemy of the people." Ten years later, Solzhenitsyn would send her a copy of his first book, *A Day in the Life of Ivan Denisovich*, with this dedication: "To the doctor who prevented me from dying."

After his cure, a new life commenced for Solzhenitsyn—a life which, in his words, "did not belong to me, [but rather] a life subordinated to an objective." It is thanks in no small measure to Irina that the epochal, history-changing *Gulag Archipelago* was to see the light of day.

Irina Meyke was one of those generous souls—and there were more of them than is generally realized—who, although raised under militant atheism, remained attentive and faithful to the voice of their consciences all their lives long.

The Orthodox priest who presided at Irina's funeral service exclaimed, "To listen to one's conscience and live according to it throughout a life lived under Communism—that is heroism!"

To listen to one's conscience and to live according to it is always heroic. Do not let your conscience be stifled by infidelity of whatever kind, comfort seeking, or a craven desire to take the path of least resistance. Living according to one's conscience is hard but it is essential to living virtuously and to leading.

In this regard, I think of a young Latvian woman who participated in a leadership seminar I gave at the University of Riga. Scantily clad and exceedingly well endowed—a kind of Latvian Marilyn Monroe, she sat in the first row with her boyfriend. I opened the session with the question: "What is leadership?" Her hand shot up and she blurted out: "Leadership is POWER!"

I gave the seminar again a year later. It took place in the same classroom, with entirely different participants—with the exception of the Latvian Marilyn Monroe from the previous year. She was back, although her appearance had undergone a metamorphosis much for the better. Her new look recalled the elegance and reserve of an Audrey Hepburn. She approached me before the session started and asked if she could have the floor at the outset. She said she wanted to explain to the assembled participants that this seminar could change their lives just as it had changed hers; that leadership is a question of character and that it requires profound effort to change oneself; that this is worth doing because the joy of achieving this transformation is immense.

"Audrey" had nothing in common with "Marilyn"—neither the clothes, nor the gait, nor the facial expression, nor the smile, nor the manner of speaking. This radical transformation—at once physical and spiritual—is the fruit of a *metanoia*, of a conversion of the heart, the mind, and the will. But most of all it is the result of listening attentively to the voice of one's conscience.

We cannot develop the moral sense if we do not listen to our conscience and obey it faithfully. Listen so as to obey, because if you do not live the way you think, you will end up thinking the way you live. We will wind up justifying the vilest actions. As Joseph Brodsky, the Soviet-born poet of Jewish ancestry and recipient of the Nobel Prize in Literature (1987), once said: "To deny God is blindness, but most times it is swinishness." One denies the highest realities because it is easier to live that way—like a pig.

Work on yourself, more than on your ideas

Good is intrinsic to man—and evil as well. Enlightenment philosophy, by denying the evil in man and focusing almost exclusively on social reform, did humanity a disservice. It formed people largely devoid of the concepts of personal development and moral perfection, people who place their hope only in social progress and politics.

As Sergei Bulgakov, the Russian philosopher, puts it: "Rousseau, and with him the entire Enlightenment, thought that . . . original sin is a superstitious myth which does not correspond to moral experience. . . . Evil is explained by the external disorder of human society, and, therefore, the task of social organization is to overcome this external disorder. There is neither personal guilt, nor personal responsibility and the whole task of social organization consists in the overcoming of this external disorder through, of course, external reforms."[1]

"Human beings are like trees in the forest," says Evgeny Bazarov, the main character in Ivan Turgeniev's novel *Fathers and Sons*. "Moral maladies are the fruit . . . of the lamentable state of society. . . . Improve society, and there will be no more maladies. . . . When society is well organized, it will no longer matter if a person is intelligent or stupid, good or bad."[2]

With its mechanistic and amoral vision of the human being, the Enlightenment philosophy has created "horizontal man," "mass man," who is a zombie incapable of conceiving of personal growth because he has long since lost the sense of his individuality and dignity.

A good example of "horizontal man" is Javert, the police inspector in Victor Hugo's *Les Miserables*. Javert obsessively enforces laws; law and order are his gods. Javert does not believe in man or his capacity for change. He believes in the system, of which he is a cog

1. S. Bulgakov, "Geroizm y podvizhnichestvo." VEHI: sbornik statej o russkoj intelligentsii, Moskva: 1909; Frankfurt: Possev, 1967.

2. I. Turgeniev, *Fathers and Sons.* Chapter 16.

in the wheel. Javert seems scarcely a person—indeed seems not to have a first name. And when Jean Valjean—through his virtue—prevails over the system, Javert leaps into the Seine and drowns.

In the ninteenth century, such writers as Nikolai Gogol and Anton Chekhov were well aware of the drama that this new conception of man and society had provoked. What is most impressive about the lives of these giants of world literature is not their *verbal* critique of Enlightenment philosophy, but the passion with which they *lived* according to diametrically opposed principles.

Gogol was not content merely to *assert* that social change is useless if people do not strive to transform their interior selves. He passed from assertion to action: "I am still building, and developing my character," he wrote to a friend. "In particular, I am now carrying out a fierce transformation of my interior self."[3]

Chekhov does more than assert his intention to change: he works hard on his interior self. As he said: "I train myself as much as possible."[4] In the view of poet Kornei Chukovsky:

> Chekhov succeeded in mastering his impulsive temperament in rooting out all that was wretched and vulgar, and acquiring a delicacy and sweetness which no other writer of his generation possessed. . . . Chekhov's noble character did not fall

3. Cf. N. Gogol, *Vybrannye mesta iz perepiski s druziami* (Sankt-Peterburg: Azbuka-Klassika, 2008), 9.

4. Cf. K. Chukovsky, *O Chekhove* (Moskva: Russkii Put', 2008), 35.

from heaven. His attractive spiritual qualities were the result of a painful interior struggle, a trophy won by hard work. . . . The remarkable independence of all of his tastes and opinions, his bold contempt for the already ossified ideals and slogans of the intelligentsia of his day, frightened his liberal critics who despotically demanded that he submit his entire *oeuvre* to their sectarian canons. One had to be a man of strong character to deal with this.[5]

Instead of placing our hope in social progress and ideology, we must strengthen our character and develop our virtues. It is a point of principle, and it says a lot about the maturity of those who adhere to it, and about the immaturity of those who, consciously or unconsciously, do not.

Work on your character, more than on your manners

I recall a case I worked on as a young lawyer. It concerned a mother, a father, and their baby boy. One day, tired of the baby's incessant screaming, they put him in the refrigerator. He died and the parents were condemned to prison. They were ordinary people: they had a house, a car, a television, a dog . . . and a baby.

Like the grossly negligent couple, we too may be attractive, well-spoken, and well-educated, and we would

---

5. Ibid., 54, 55, 70.

certainly never commit such a heinous crime. But are our hearts really purer, our moral sense more acute?

Many people strive to improve their looks and the way they present themselves, but neglect to work on their character, and fail to develop a moral sense. Catherine the Great, the German princess who became Empress of Russia (1762–1796), corresponds to this type. The eminent Russian historian Vasily Klyuchevsky paints this portrait:

> Catherine developed in herself attributes of high, day-to-day value. . . . Frequent self-examination kept her in a constant state of mobilization. . . . She demonstrated an incomparable ability to listen patiently to all manner of twaddle, gingerly helping tongue-tied interlocutors find the right word. This won people over, got them to open up, inspired confidence. . . . To a high degree, she possessed an artful mastery of what may be called the power of suggestion—not having to give an order but to express a desire, which, in the impressionable mind, is imperceptibly reborn as its own idea and is carried out with enthusiasm. . . . But Catherine developed the habit of working on her manners, rather than on her feelings. . . . The insufficiency of her moral formation propelled her away from the correct path of development, on which she had been placed by her happy nature, . . . She perceived in herself weaknesses without any pangs of conscience, without any impulse to pity or remorse. . . . The tree of

self-knowledge, if deprived of the moral sense, yields
the unhealthy fruit of self-conceit. . . . A creature
of the intellect who gave no quarter to the heart,
Catherine's actions had a surface brilliance, but rarely
achieved greatness or demonstrated creativity.[6]

It is worth reflecting on this portrait of Catherine. It could serve as an examination of conscience for us. This is a portrait of mediocrity masquerading as "greatness." It is also the portrait of all those who, because they lack a moral sense, are incapable of growing in virtue, and find themselves obliged to lead not by character (which they do not possess), but by human relations techniques that often degenerate into manipulation. And the result is always the same—lots of sound and fury, but little greatness and creativity. An absence of authentic leadership, one might say.

It is remarkable that Catherine, called "the Great," had arrested, tortured, and sent into exile some of the genuinely great people of her generation, such as Nikolai Novikov and Alexander Radishchev, Russian writers and philanthropists who publicly criticized serfdom and aimed to improve the cultural and educational level of the Russian people. Novikov and Radishchev were men of character. History remembers them for their magnanimity, whereas it remembers Catherine for her selfishness.

---

6. V. O. Klyuchevsky, *Istoria Rossii*. Chapter 75.

CHAPTER 4

Developing Magnanimity

Let us now reflect on the means by which to grow in magnanimity.

◇   ◇   ◇

Seek out a man, a true man

To grow in magnanimity, we should seek the company of magnificent people who are conscious of their dignity and manifest it in the way they live. Diogenes went about in broad daylight with an illuminated lantern, crying out, "I am looking for a man, a true man." We should do the same, forging friendships with people who inspire us by their luminous personal qualities, above all, their magnanimity.

While it may seem that we rarely encounter truly magnanimous people, we may know more such people than we think.

A participant in a leadership seminar I gave in Alma-Ata, Kazakhstan, once asked me: "Tell us, Alexander, who, in your opinion, are the greatest leaders?"

The group probably expected me to name the usual suspects—Churchill, de Gaulle, Gandhi, and Steve Jobs. I hesitated a moment, then answered with deep conviction: "My parents!" My interlocutor did not expect this answer. I could tell my answer had thrown him for a loop. But a few seconds later he and the entire class gave me a rousing ovation. It was an ovation for ordinary life!

In discovering the greatness in those around us, we must take a positive approach to life and recognize that everyone has his or her strengths and weaknesses. We must learn to filter events through our memory so as to remember only the positive things. Like a Georgian *tamada*,[1] who, with poetry and humor, and without resorting to flattery, raises a toast to the greatness of his guests, we should keep in our hearts the most beautiful memories and images of those who accompany us along the highways and byways of life.

The first ones to accompany us are our parents, our grandparents, our brothers and sisters. In the lines that follow, I will be the *tamada*, and my guests will be the members of my family. As you read them, place yourself in the traditional role of the Georgian *tamada*, and generously toast those nearest and dearest to you.

My father is called Cyril. The name means "lordly" in Greek. My father is a great lord, a man without limits, a man with a big spirit. An avid sailor, he is not at peace unless he is sailing the seas. For his lack of

---

1. A *tamada* is a Georgian master of ceremonies, or toastmaster.

restraint, which corresponds to his Russian soul, some love him and some despise him. When he is not terrorizing the Parisian *beau monde*, he is at his home in Transcaucasia reveling in the fresh mountain air and writing his memoirs.

My mother is called Irene. The name means "peaceful" in Greek. My mother, however, is anything but peaceful. Hers is a fiery temperament. She is always at war. And when she loves, she loves to the very end. Hundreds of young people in times of hardship found a refuge in her motherly heart. The most impressive thing about her is her faithfulness.

Madeleine is my maternal grandmother. She fondly recalls her father who was a French army officer. When she was a little girl at the turn of the last century, her father would ride through the streets of Paris on horseback with Madeleine perched in front of him. She has a fiery temperament like her daughter (my mother). She loves God, and she is the one who taught me to pray. In the 1930s, she married my grandfather Artchil, a Georgian aristocrat who had fled the Communist regime. Artchil is the epitome of manly goodness and kindness. He forged his character in suffering. When he sees us—his grandchildren—he devours us with his smile and the welcoming look in his eyes.

Nina is my paternal grandmother. She was born in Saint Petersburg. In 1920, at the age of eighteen, she fled Russia with her parents and two sisters. Nina is all sweetness and light. She gave me the language of her native land. She loves reading Chekhov more than anything else. She married Pavel in Paris. He was a young Russian immigrant who had lost his parents in the Civil War that followed the Bolshevik seizure of power. His only assets were his high intelligence and innate serenity. He knows how to listen to people and makes the effort to understand them. Many people seek his counsel.

Stephen is my brother. He is not made for this world. He spends his days hovering above the earth with his parachute, or in the depths of the sea with his oxygen tanks. He is a man of action. He is a great athlete, intellectual, and poet. If he had lived in ancient times, he would have been Alexander the Great.

My sister Mary is everything a woman would dream of being. At seventeen, she left the warmth and comfort of our home to serve the poor in the slums that ring Paris. She is the heroine of my youth. If she had lived in the Middle Ages, she would have been Joan of Arc.[2] I spent my youth surrounded by people of remarkable moral, intellectual, and physical qualities. I often think of my parents, grandparents, brother, and sister. I find in them examples of greatness lived in daily life.

Tolstoy's *Anna Karenina* begins with these words: "Happy families are all alike; every unhappy family is unhappy in its own way." My experience tells me the opposite is true: happiness is always original because

---

2. As I write these lines, the members of my family mentioned above have passed away, all except for my father Cyril and my sister Mary.

it is the fruit of love and virtue, which are always new and creative; unhappiness is monotonous, just as a life without love and virtue is monotonous.

Once, a participant in one of my leadership seminars approached me and said: "My father abandoned me before I was even born. My mother was a bad mother and we have no relationship. Where do you want me to go to find greatness?"

We cannot choose our parents, but we can fill the moral vacuum created by their shortcomings by seeking out virtuous friends. The first step is to acknowledge to yourself the absence of positive influences in your life and then to take decisive action to rectify the situation. Acknowledging the problem and determining to act is probably the most significant act of leadership one can make. We are free to choose our friends, and if we choose them well, they can have a positive influence on us that surpasses even that of our parents.

In my first year of law school in Paris, I made the acquaintance of Maxime, a student who had two great passions in life: Bruce Lee and the Virgin Mary. We quickly became great friends. Often, after class, we would go either to a Bruce Lee movie, or to the Cathedral of Notre Dame to visit Our Lady. One day, Maxime invited me to a center of Opus Dei near the rue Mozart, where he introduced me to Xavier, the center's director. Xavier was twenty years our senior, a professor of history at the Sorbonne, and one of the world's leading experts on the Mexican revolution. Xavier soon became my mentor and spiritual director. He exerted an enormous, positive influence on me through his paternal concern for my interior life, his professional example and his friendship. It was he who helped me to understand the words of Saint Paul: "What no eye has seen, nor ear heard, nor the heart of man conceived, what God has prepared for those who love him."[3] It was he who made me discover my vocation.

Friends cannot replace parents, but there comes a time in life when friends are more important than parents.

We find greatness among our loved ones and our friends. We also find it in people we meet as we go through life. And when we do, we should not keep our distance. We should contemplate them, study them, admire their virtues and seek to imitate them.

Let beauty penetrate your spirit

There are masterpieces of world culture in which ethics and aesthetics coincide in such a manner as to propel us to unexpected emotional heights. The resulting euphoria helps us shake off complacency, mediocrity, and our bourgeois ways of being. Such works reveal the greatness of man and give rise to a thirst for life, for accomplishing great things, for self-sacrifice.

After reading *Joan of Arc* by Mark Twain (an untypical work for Twain, but the one he considered his best), I had the same sensation as I had after reading Dostoyevsky's *Crime and Punishment*—a sensation of

---

3. 1 Corinthians 2:9.

euphoria. Joan of Arc and Sonya Marmeladova evoke in me powerful emotions similar to the ones I feel when I contemplate a beautiful icon of the Mother of God.

I think also of several movies which touched me deeply: *The Mirror* by Andrei Tarkovsky, *Chariots of Fire* by Hugh Hudson, *The Deer Hunter* by Michael Cimino. I think of the songs of Jacques Brel, whose bracing lyrics are like a slap in the face.

I think of the liturgical chant "Praise the Lord, O my Soul" from Rachmaninov's *All-Night Vigil*, with Klara Korkan as the female soloist.[4] It is a paean to the beauty and greatness of God's creation. Years ago, friends and I would spend summer nights on the shores of the Atlantic. We would listen to Korkan's voice, rapt, as it mingled with the crashing of the waves and ascended to the moonlit sky above, and we found ourselves imbued with the power and the glory of God.

It is through aesthetics that ethics—that is to say, the virtues—will regain the force they have lost in modern times. "Beauty will save the world,"[5] says Dostoyevsky, because it is the most complete and immediate expression of Truth and Goodness. Everyone has his own artistic tastes, but we are all called to let ourselves be penetrated by beauty and to respond to it appropriately.

---

4. Cf. S. Rachmaninoff, Opus 37, "Bless the Lord, O My Soul" (Greek Chant), Alexander Sveshnikov, Klara Korkan, Konstantin Ognevoi & State Russian Choir.

5. Cf. F. Dostoyevsky, *The Idiot*.

Discover your vocation and live it

Letting the opportunity pass, not seizing it out of fear or laziness—this is what makes a magnanimous soul suffer more than anything else. *For the magnanimous person, evil is not something done by others; it is the good that he, personally, did not do.*

We must be responsible people. To be responsible is to respond personally and generously to the "call of humanity," with all of one's heart and mind and will.

We are called to reject selfishness, and live in solidarity with other people. This is the "call of humanity." It is addressed to all people everywhere. But there is another call, one more specific and personal, and that is the call of vocation. A vocation is a divine call: it is God who is calling each and every one of us, and calling us by our name.

Everyone has a vocation, whether he knows it or not. A vocation is a call to live, think, and act in a particular way. It is the criterion according to which we measure all of our actions; it is the principle that gives unity to our lives.

If the "call of humanity" is a call addressed to the conscience, the call of God is addressed to the heart. The call of God is more intimate than the "call of humanity." He who does not hear the "call of humanity" will have trouble hearing the call of God. By the same token, he who hears the "call of humanity" and responds to it generously is primed to hear the call of God.

To respond to the call of God is an act of theological hope because we trust that God *will give us* the means to act and be faithful to our vocation. But, in the first instance, it is an act of magnanimity because we trust in the gifts God *has already given us*, and are thankful for them.

I am always astonished when people who have grown up in stable families and received lots of human, moral, and cultural formation turn their backs on their vocation, while others who had difficult upbringings in unstable homes and received little positive formation nevertheless discover their vocation and live it with exemplary fidelity. The "rich young man" of the New Testament—pious and from a good home[6]—rejects the call of God, whereas Mary Magdalene, the woman possessed by seven demons,[7] generously embraces her vocation when she discovers it. They make an impression on us—the one for his smallness of heart, the other for her magnanimity. It is often the case that the small of heart underestimate the value of what they have received, while the magnanimous believe that what little they have received is of inestimable value.

Take the case of Esa, a Finnish journalist. I met him in 1990 when he was 45. He had not had an easy life. His father, an alcoholic, drowned when Esa was very young. His mother was incapable of raising him and his brother properly. The brother ran away from home and joined Jehovah's Witnesses. After finishing school in the revolutionary year of 1968, Esa moved to

---

6. Cf. Matthew 19:16–30.
7. Cf. Luke 8:2.

East Berlin, the capital of the Soviet-aligned German Democratic Republic. Esa signed on as a spy for the Stasi, the GDR's secret police force.

Esa had not lost his bearings; he never had any in the first place.

A few years later, in the 1970s, Esa had a chance encounter with a childhood friend while on a brief visit to Helsinki, the capital of Finland. The encounter changed his life. His friend's personal warmth, the power of his words, and his human concern started a process of transformation in the secret agent's heart. It took a matter of hours.

Esa confessed publicly at a packed press conference in a hotel in central Finland. He then turned himself in to the police. He received a suspended prison sentence of six months. After his chance encounter with an old friend in the streets of Helsinki, his life turned around. He responded generously to his Christian vocation. He appreciated the exalted value of the gift he had received—the gift of conversion.

Be aware of your talent and increase it

Eric Liddell was aware of his talent: "I believe that God created me for a purpose, but he also made me fast." Liddell had a missionary vocation and he was aware of it, and it was as a missionary that he died in 1945 in a Japanese concentration camp in Manchuria. But he was also aware of his speed, a talent he had no intention of letting go to waste. At the 1924 Olympic games in Paris, he refused, on religious grounds, to compete in his specialty—the 100 meters—because the race was being run on a Sunday. But that did not prevent him from training for several months to compete in other races and from breaking the world record in the 400 meters and winning the Gold Medal.

Like Eric Liddell, the American writer Flannery O'Connor was aware of her talent. When she was asked before a large audience why she wrote, she replied without hesitation: "Because I write well!" Her audience expressed its (pharisaical) disapproval of what it construed to be her pride, but she was expressing her magnanimity and nothing else. She understood that her audience did not understand and that made her laugh with perfect simplicity.[8]

What am I good at? What is my strength? It is not always clear. "Most people," said Peter Drucker, "think they know what they are good at. They are usually wrong. . . . There is only one way to find out: Feedback Analysis."[9] It is hard to know what we are good at before the age of 25, or even 30. We should explore many avenues and also ask our friends or colleagues to help us discover what we are really good at.

Having identified our talent, we then need to develop it. *Although it is important to overcome our weaknesses, it is much more important to develop our strengths.*

---

8. Cf. G.W. Shepherd, *The Example of Flannery O'Connor as a Christian Writer* (Center Journal, Winter), 1984.

9. P. Drucker, *Management Challenges for the 21st Century* (New York: HarperCollins Publishers, 2001), 164, 179.

Concentrate your energies on your mission

In *Virtuous Leadership* I used the words "vocation" and "mission" almost interchangeably. Here I would like to differentiate between them. Vocation is a call to *being*, whereas mission is a call to *doing*. Vocation is a call *to be a certain way*; mission is a call *to do a certain thing*. Vocation is always a divine call, whereas a mission is often the result of human considerations.

Our vocation is the framework in which we discover and carry out our mission, which constitutes our specific contribution to humanity. Without a vocation, leadership is *devoid of purpose*; without a mission, it is *devoid of substance*.

Many have a clear sense of their vocation, but have trouble discovering their mission. This is because they are insufficiently aware of their talent or insufficiently imaginative. Conversely, many understand that they have a mission, but are not aware that they have a vocation. This is because their religious sense is insufficiently developed.

Once we have identified our mission, we must devote all of our energy to carrying it out. In 1963, two Orthodox priests—Aleksandr Men and Dmitriy Dudko—visited the Russian writer Aleksandr Solzhenitsyn at his home in the provincial city of Ryazan. Solzhenitsyn had just written *A Day in the Life of Ivan Denisovich*, the work that would launch his public career. Twenty years later, Men recalled:

> Solzhenitsyn was a fascinating human being. He grasped ideas and understood complexities

immediately. . . . He was a very lively interlocutor, but I noted that he was focused exclusively on the themes that interested him. I'm not criticizing him for it and in fact welcome it: he was able to let all sorts of things sail past him with indifference, but as soon as he heard words that served the function of signal flares for him, he would immediately spring to life. When Father Dudko mentioned that he had been an inmate in a particular camp, Solzhenitsyn was all ears, wanting to know all the details, which he immediately entered into his notebook.[10]

Everyone has his own unique mission, which he discovers when he becomes aware of his talent. The accomplishment of this mission requires all of our vital energies.

Do not be afraid of failure

The inverse of magnanimity is pusillanimity. It is the mistaken belief that we are incapable of great things. As such, it is rooted in the fear of failure. Fear engenders despair, and despair paralyzes the soul, impeding its ability to achieve great things.

Despair is a vice. It is worse than the vice of presumption (believing yourself to be capable of something when you are not), because it condemns man to mediocrity and decline.

---

10. S.S. Bytchkov, *KGB protiv sviachtchennika Aleksandra Menia, www. portal-credo.ru*, 2010.

It was because she overcame her fear of failure that Maria Callas scaled new professional heights. In 1949, Maestro Tullio Serafin asked her to replace Margherita Carosio, who had fallen ill, in the role of Elvira in Bellini's *I Puritani*. He gave Callas six days to learn the role. Callas protested that this was impossible. Not only was the role entirely new to her, she was already under contract to sing the role of Bruennhilde in Wagner's *The Valkyrie* three times a week. Callas was convinced she was not up to the challenge. Serafin reassured her: "I guarantee you can do it."[11]

In the briefest amount of time Callas mastered one of the most complex roles in the repertory, submitting her voice to enormous pressure. "What she did . . . was really incredible," said Franco Zeffirelli, the famous opera and film director. "You need to be familiar with opera to realize the dimensions of her achievement. It was as if someone had asked Birgit Nilsson, who is famous for her great Wagnerian voice, to substitute overnight for Beverly Sills, who is one of the great coloratura sopranos of our time."[12]

Callas' dramatic portrayal of Elvira stunned the musical world and made her, overnight, a star of international renown. She would go on to transform opera through her talent not merely as a singer but as an actress. Thanks to her acting ability, she was able to

---

11. *Callas: In Her Own Words* (Audio Cassette).

12. D. A. Lowe, *Callas: As They Saw Her* (New York: Ungar Publishing Company, 1986).

incarnate the characters she was interpreting. In the words of Montserrat Caballé: "She opened a new door for us, for all singers in the world, a door that had been closed. Behind it was sleeping not only great music, but interpretation as well. She has given us the chance to do things that were hardly possible before."[13]

By overcoming her fear of failure, Maria Callas attained new professional heights and made a signal contribution to the art of opera.

Free your imagination

Fueled perhaps by their dreams of hatred and destruction, demonic personalities often possess powerful imaginations. In August 1914, Vladimir Lenin, viewing the bloody, mangled bodies of wounded soldiers transiting the railway station at Krakov, understood instantly what was needed to set Communism on the path to power: the Great War must drag on as long as possible—pushing the limits of human suffering—to the point where it would become transformed into a civil war that would bring down governments across Europe.

Not only the devils, but also the saints often possess powerful imaginations. It was in September of 1946 that Mother Teresa received the great inspiration of her life in a railway carriage bound for Darjeeling while contemplating the poverty all around her—to become a

---

13. J. Ardoin, G. Fitzgerald, *Callas: The Art and the Life* (New York: Holt, Rinehart and Winston), 1974.

mother to the poorest of the world's poor, to share their interior desolation, to demonstrate to the entire world the infinite love of God for each and every person.

Lenin's imagination is the fruit of hatred, exacerbated by satanic intervention; Teresa's is the fruit of love, transfigured by God's grace.

Love must be the driving force behind imagination. Love for flesh-and-blood people, but also love for the material world created by God. We must passionately love all the good and noble things in the world. Marius Mignol, the inventor of the radial tire, was passionately in love with pneumatic engineering. "If you are not passionate about the tire," he once said to a young colleague—François Michelin—who eventually became his boss, "you have no business working at Michelin."[14]

François Michelin, who, in the course of the next 45 years, would lead his firm from tenth-ranked to the world's largest, assimilated the lesson straight away. He became passionate about tires and was a great inventor in his own right. René Zingraff, a former senior executive at Michelin, said of him: "What made François Michelin stand out was his imagination. He was highly imaginative. You had to hear him talking to his researchers, pushing them to see farther. He opened new horizons."[15]

Love must be the driving force of imagination, but for the imagination to be fertile, you have to devote

---

14. Interview with F. Michelin by A. Havard, January 20, 2010.

15. "Michelin—Son histoire."

time to it. You have to know how to "waste time" with your imagination. You have to nourish it, give it free rein, and push it to its limits.

Reject hedonism

Pusillanimity is triumphant in the modern world. This is a consequence of the regnant hedonist culture, which does profound psychic harm to adolescents, robbing them of all sense of the moral greatness of life.

For many young people, this phase of life, which psychiatrists call "romantic," is anything but. The cult of pleasure and the over-sexualization of Western culture have deprived young people of all sense of romance, idealism, and life's inherent nobility. Many young people lack any orientation to that which comes from above, and are less prone than ever before to dream of great and noble deeds, becoming instead calculating, evasive, and manipulative.

In his *Picture of Dorian Gray*, Oscar Wilde describes with profound realism the shrinking, indeed the disintegrating, heart of a young man given to hedonism. Lust destroys all sense of greatness in man.

As noted above, magnanimity comes easier to young people than to older ones. But the passage of time is not the only way to age in the modern world. Getting caught up in the cult of sex will age you before your time by deadening your soul. There are plenty of aged people walking around who are still in their teens.

Reject all forms of egalitarianism

The triumph of pusillanimity is also the fruit of an egalitarian mentality that abhors any hint of aristocracy or superiority of whatever kind.

The celebrated speech of Callicles in Plato's *Gorgias* contains some important truths: It is to "frighten the most powerful, the most capable of overpowering them, and preventing them from winning," that the masses reject superiority, calling it "bad and unjust," and insisting that "injustice consists essentially in the desire to rise above the others." That is why "we form the best and the strongest among us, taking them at a young age, like lion cubs, for us to enslave by means of childish tricks telling them that no one should have more than anyone else, and that in this consists justice, and beauty."[16]

It is a very positive thing to want to be a member of the intellectual, commercial, artistic, or sporting elite of one's country or the world. To want to be a member of the elite *so as to serve others as effectively as possible*— that is an act of magnanimity.

In their dignity, human beings are radically equal, but in their talents, they are radically unequal. There is something demonic in the quest for equality at any cost. Dostoyevsky understood this when he had one of his *possessed* say the following:

> Everyone belongs to all and all belong to everyone.
> All are slaves and equal in their slavery. . . . To

---

16. Platon, *Gorgias* 483 a.

begin with, the level of education, science and talents is lowered. A high level of education and science is possible only to great intellects, and they are not wanted. . . . They will be banished or put to death. Cicero will have his tongue cut out, Copernicus will have his eyes put out, and Shakespeare will be stoned. . . . Slaves will be bound to be equal.[17]

In the spirit of Dostoyevsky, Antoine de Saint-Exupéry violently criticized this egalitarian temptation, which "assassinates Mozart," transforming people and whole nations into little better than animals in a fattening farm.

Egalitarianism, like lust, destroys in man his very sense of greatness.

Seek greatness in ordinary life

Nothing is greater than God. He is hidden in the most banal situations. Here are the words of Vladimir Soloviev, the philosopher and poet:

Not trusting in this deceptive world,
Under the mundane guise of matter,
I touched the imperishable purple
And recognized the splendor of divinity.[18]

---

17. F. Dostoyevsky, *The Possessed*, vol. 2, chapter 8 ("Ivan the Tsarevich").
18. V. Soloviev, *Three Encounters*.

This is what Saint Josemaria Escriva, an experienced pastor of souls, tells us:

> God waits for us everyday in the laboratory, in the operating theater, in the army barracks, in the university chair, in the factory, in the workshop, in the fields, in the home, and in all the immense panorama of work. Understand this well: there is something holy, something divine, hidden in the most ordinary situations, and it is up to everyone of you to discover it.[19]

Too often we seek greatness in extraordinary feats and impossible dreams. We expect to find greatness at some future date and in some other place. We fail to understand that greatness is to be achieved here and now in the immediate, tangible reality of our material surroundings.

The Author of all creation, the magnanimous Being *par excellence*, he who "is able to do far more abundantly than all that we ask or think,"[20] abides in ordinary life.

To abandon the ordinary in favor of the extraordinary is to seek oneself rather than God. It is to seek glory and amusement rather than virtue. It can bring a quick halt to one's personal development.

---

19. J. Escrivá, *Conversations with Monsignor Josemaría Escrivá* (New York: Scepter Publishers, 2003), no. 114.

20. Ephesians 3:20.

The historian Vasily Klyuchevsky composed this portrait of Patriarch Nikon, an important personage in seventeenth century Russia, whose ill-considered reforms led to a dramatic and lasting schism in the Russian Orthodox Church:

> In ordinary life, he was ponderous, flighty, irascible, ambitious, and, above all, vain. . . . He could calmly bear unspeakable sufferings, but would despair of a pinprick. . . . Calm bored him, he found it impossible to wait patiently; he needed constant tension, bold ideas and great undertakings. . . . He was like a sail that only functioned in storms, but in periods of calm was just a useless rag fluttering from a mast.[21]

A useless rag suspended from a mast—hardly the image of an authentic leader. Authentic leadership is based not on feelings and external stimuli, but on the virtues that are stable habits of the personality. *If one is not a leader at all times, one is not a leader at all.*

Abraham Lincoln is a classical example of a man who was a leader at all times. He never made any distinction between that which is ordinary and that which is extraordinary. "He brought to every question,— the loftiest and most imposing,—the same patient inquiry into details, the same eager longing to know and do exactly what was just and right, and the same

---

21. V. Klyuchevsky, op cit., chapter 54.

working-day, plodding, laborious devotion, which characterized his management of a client's case at his law office in Springfield. He had duties to perform in both places—in the one case to his country, as to his client in the other. But all duties were alike to him. All called equally upon him for the best service of his mind and heart, and all were alike performed with a conscientious, single-hearted devotion that knew no distinction, but was absolute and perfect in every case."[22]

Lincoln was so much the man of the ordinary that his friend Joseph Gillespie could write: "Mr. Lincoln was a great common man. He was a giant but formed and fashioned like other men. He only differed from most men in degree. He had only their qualities but then he had them in larger measure than any man of modern times."[23]

To seek to achieve greatness through the fulfillment of ordinary responsibilities is one thing; to fail to respond to opportunities to help mankind is quite another. Many people are so wrapped up in ordinary affairs that they are unaware of the extraordinary talents they possess, and the extraordinary responsibility that goes with them.

---

22. Henry Raymond, *The Life, Public Services, and State Papers of Abraham Lincoln*, Volume II, 723–724.

23. Howard K. Beale, editor, *The Diary of Edward Bates, 1859–1866*, (*February 26, 1863*), 281

CHAPTER 5
Growing in Humility

Let us now consider how to grow in humility.

In order to grow in humility, one must first understand the amplitude of this virtue.

Humility in its proper sense is the *habit of living in the truth.* To live in the truth is to recognize one's status as a creature (metaphysical humility), as well as one's natural weaknesses and personal faults (spiritual humility). It is also to recognize one's dignity and greatness (ontological humility) as well as one's talent and virtue (psychological humility). Finally, it is to recognize the dignity and greatness of others (fraternal humility).

Humility is the fruit of the knowledge of God, of the knowledge of self, and of the knowledge of others.

Acknowledge your nothingness (metaphysical humility)

To practice humility is, first of all, to acknowledge one's status as a creature: without God we are nothing, we do not exist. God created us out of nothing and maintains us in being. If He were to stop thinking about us for even a second, we would be transformed into non-being in that very instant. Autonomous man, man independent of God, is pure nothingness.

Humility is a *religious* virtue. It is the natural attitude of the creature before the Creator. The Greek philosophers had no real concept of humility. If they failed to grasp the concept outright, it is because they lacked a true idea of God, of his transcendence and creative power, God who gives life and sustains it every instant, thereby justifying the humble prayer of his creature, man.

In acknowledging our nothingness, we acknowledge the greatness of God who gives us being. In doing so, we achieve interior peace and the confidence to act because we know that this God is not just God the Creator, but also "the Father of mercies and God of all comfort"[1] who is All Powerful.

People who pride themselves on their independence and autonomy—on being, in effect, gods—cannot achieve peace because every day, indeed, every moment of every day, they experience their flaws and limitations. Happiness without God is a contradiction in terms.

---

1. 2 Corinthians 1:3.

Acknowledge your weakness (spiritual humility)

To practice humility is to acknowledge "this some-thing which fights against reason and resists it,"[2] which Christians call concupiscence—the triple tendency towards pleasure, affluence, and power, a result of the disorder introduced in human nature by original sin.

It is a potentially grave mistake to refuse to acknowledge this disorder, for he who does not know the cause of evil, will not know the remedy. This would be tragic because there is a remedy at hand, namely, the assiduous practice of the natural virtues, along with the supernatural ones, which come to us through prayer and the sacraments instituted by Christ.

One day, I presented François Michelin a copy of the French edition of *Virtuous Leadership*. Looking at the cover, he smiled broadly and said: "This is all fine, but if you do not speak of original sin in this book, you won't get very far: it would be like not having the instruction manual." Michelin was happily surprised when I said: "But I do speak of it, sir. I speak of it a lot."

Spiritual humility also recognizes personal trans-gressions against virtue and the natural moral law. The Judeo-Christian tradition calls these faults *sins* because they are offenses against God, the Creator of man and the Author of the natural law.

The modern world's loss of the sense of sin stems from its loss of the sense of God. If there is no God,

---

2. Aristotle, *Nicomachean Ethics*, 1102 b 14–28.

he cannot be offended. There are only "crimes against humanity," crimes against man. Sin is obviously an offense against humanity: it harms both the sinner (who is made in the image of God) and the one who is sinned against. But sin is also, and, above all, an offense against God.

To practice humility, finally, is to acknowledge one's mistakes. We should not be afraid of them; they are not offenses against God. But we should learn from our mistakes. "The number of mistakes that I have made and which this company has been kind enough to help me notice," says François Michelin, "has been considerable. But without this, I would never have grown."[3]

Recognize your dignity and greatness (ontological humility)

To recognize one's dignity and personal greatness is not just an act of magnanimity, it's also an act of humility, because it brings us closer to the truth about ourselves.

Man in himself is pure nothingness, but man created in the image of God, man ransomed by the Son and divinized by the Holy Spirit, is truly a miracle. Every human being is God's offspring, his son or daughter. Whoever is not aware of his divine sonship "ignores his most intimate truth."[4]

By his reason, man understands that he is not just a material being but also a spiritual one, because he

---

3. "Michelin—Son histoire."

4. J. Escrivá, *Friends of God* (New York: Scepter Publishers, 1981), no. 26.

possesses a rational intelligence and free will. He is aware of the strength of his spirit and of his heart.

But man is incapable of understanding himself by reason alone. He does not know who he is. It is God who enables him to understand himself: "And because you are sons . . . [I purified you] from all unrighteousness . . . no eye has seen, nor ear heard, nor the heart of man conceived, what God has prepared for those who love him."[5] God reveals to man his dignity and his eternal destiny.

Man discovers who he is and the ultimate meaning of his life through faith. Faith is essential to the practice of humility, which is the habit of living in the truth.

Acknowledge your talents and use them (psychological humility)

To acknowledge one's talents is an act of magnanimity. It is also an act of humility because it brings us closer to the truth about ourselves. *We must have the humility to acknowledge our talents.*

In acknowledging our talents, we thank God, who created us. Not to acknowledge our talents is not humility; it is ingratitude.

We need to acknowledge our talents before we can make use of them. God imposes a penalty on those

---

5. Cf. Galatians 4:6; 1 John 1:9; 1 Corinthians 2:9.

who, in the name of a *false humility*, refuse to make use of their talents. To quote our Lord:

> "A man going on a journey called his servants and entrusted to them his property; to one he gave five talents, to another two, to another one, to each according to his ability. Then he went away. He who had received the five talents went at once and traded with them; and he made five talents more. So also, he who had the two talents made two talents more. But he who had received the one talent went and dug in the ground and hid his master's money. Now after a long time the master of those servants came and settled accounts with them. And he who had received the five talents came forward, bringing five talents more, saying, 'Master, you delivered to me five talents; here I have made five talents more.' His master said to him, 'Well done, good and faithful servant; you have been faithful over a little, I will set you over much; enter into the joy of your master.' And he also who had the two talents came forward, saying, 'Master, you delivered to me two talents; here I have made two talents more.' His master said to him, 'Well done, good and faithful servant; you have been faithful over a little, I will set you over much; enter into the joy of your master.' He also who had received the one talent came forward, saying, 'Master, I knew you to be a hard man, reaping where you did not sow, and gathering

where you did not winnow; so I was afraid, and I went and hid your talent in the ground. Here you have what is yours.' But his master answered him, 'You wicked and slothful servant! You knew that I reap where I have not sowed, and gather where I have not winnowed? Then you ought to have invested my money with the bankers, and at my coming I should have received what was my own with interest. So take the talent from him, and give it to him who has the ten talents. For to every one who has will more be given, and he will have abundance; but from him who has not, even what he has will be taken away. And cast the worthless servant into the outer darkness; there men will weep and gnash their teeth.'"[6]

This parable, known as the "parable of the talents," makes perfectly clear the difference between humility and pusillanimity. A humble person is not afraid of his talents, but rather of failing to make good use of them. The pusillanimous person, by contrast, fears making use of his talents: he digs a hole and buries them in it (and himself along with them).

While acknowledging our talents we should refrain from comparing ourselves to others, because we are not all equally talented, and because people differ in the specific talents they possess.

---

6. Matthew 25:14–30.

Recognize the dignity and greatness of others (fraternal humility)

Of humility's various aspects, *fraternal* humility is the one most directly relevant to leadership. Fraternal humility is the habit of serving.

If metaphysical humility is the *foundation* of humility, fraternal humility constitutes its *summit*. Fraternal humility implies metaphysical humility (which allows us to see the *presence* of God in others) and ontological humility (which allows us to see the *face* of God in others). *One cannot serve man if one does not know who man is. One can only serve man in light of the truth about man.*

If it is true that atrocities have been committed in the name of God, even worse atrocities have been committed in the name of man. Was not Communism, with its dictatorship of the proletariat and its totalitarian project to abolish the family, religion, and private property,[7] hailed as a great humanist experiment and the very fulfillment of human history? Is not the blood-soaked French Revolution endlessly hailed as a positive manifestation of humanism? It is remarkable that only four years separate the Declaration of the Rights of Man and of the Citizen (1789) and the Reign of Terror (1793). If one does not know who man is, it is easy to turn the "rights of man" against man himself. Today, the policies of many governments concerning life (abortion, euthanasia, the cloning of

---

7. Cf. K. Marx and F. Engels, *The Communist Manifesto*.

human embryos, the adoption of children by homosexual couples) demonstrate that next to nothing has changed. The word "man" remains an abstraction. And the chief victim of abstracted man is man as he really is—real man—man made in the image and likeness of God. Let me repeat: we cannot serve man if we do not know him, and we can only know him in the light of God's truth about him.

If fraternal humility implies metaphysical and ontological humility, it also implies spiritual humility, which makes us aware of the need to perfect ourselves in order to better serve others, and psychological humility, which allows us to appreciate the strengths and talents that should be put in the service of others.

To practice humility is to live for others, but also to joyously know that others exist to serve you, to accept that they have something to offer you, something intimate and personal.

The Russian poet Olga Sedakova, who knew Pope John Paul II well, once remarked: "He needed something personal from everyone he met. . . . He looked at people with such interest and hope, as if to say, 'What wonderful things will you help me discover today, what gift will you give me?'"[8]

When a leader practices humility, he teaches and inspires the people he leads. By the same token, he learns from them, and comes to see them as gifts.

---

8. O. Sedakova, *Dni Ioanna Pavla II* (Moskva: Obshestvo Ioanna Pavla II, 2008), 28.

Through them he grows and perfects himself as a human being.

Thus, to practice humility is to serve others and to allow others to serve you. Humility is to serve your family and friends, your colleagues and clients, and let yourself be served by them. Numerous are those who, through a lack of humility, do not want or do not know how to be served. As a result, they prevent others from realizing themselves as persons.

CONCLUSION

In *Virtuous Leadership*, I explained that leadership is not a matter of technique, but of *character*, a matter of virtue. In *Created for Greatness*, I have endeavored to go further: I have tried to demonstrate that leadership is *a life ideal* because the specific virtues it draws on—magnanimity and humility—are themselves life ideals. Magnanimity and humility exalt the truth about man. They are virtues that embrace the totality of his existence and bring about the flourishing of his personality.

No one is born magnanimous and humble; no one is born a leader. Leadership is the result of a free choice and diligent effort. "The world is full of men whose youthful promise of excellence has turned into middle-aged mediocrity," says Peter Drucker. By the same token, according to Drucker, "It is full of men who started out as pedestrian plodders only to blossom out into star performers in their forties. To try to appraise a man's long-range potential is a worse gamble than to try to break the bank at Monte Carlo; and the more 'scientific' the system, the greater the gamble."[1]

We cannot know how the spiritual lives of those we care about will develop, for the simple reason that

---

1. P. Drucker, *The Practice of Management* (Oxford: Elsevier, 2005), 150.

people are free. We cannot foresee the course of our own spiritual development, let alone anyone else's. We can only strive to make good choices—magnanimous and humble ones—and stick to them courageously.

◇   ◇   ◇

POSTSCRIPT 1—Practical steps

So far, I have given *essential pointers* on how to achieve greatness. Here are some of the *practical steps* to follow: 1) spiritual direction, 2) living a "plan of life," and 3) the examination of conscience.

Allow me to define these concepts:

1. *Spiritual direction.* We should seek among our close friends an advisor of wisdom and piety able to help us set short- and long-term goals. Clearly, it requires humility to accept the very idea of spiritual direction. But without spiritual direction, we cannot move forward. Excellence is not a hard and fast technique. Individuals cannot be formed on a mass basis. A book can give orientation and prompt reflection but it cannot impart the effects of spiritual direction. Each person needs to receive advice adapted to the specifics of his own soul and personal circumstances. This is the work of the spiritual director. A good director must practice the virtue of prudence in developing deep insight into the spiritual life of the person he is

advising, and in working out a realistic and demanding plan of action.

2. *The plan of life*. This comprises spiritual exercises some of which are practiced daily and some weekly, but always on a priority basis. It requires considerable discipline to follow such a plan. This is not always easy, but one will never become a leader if one is incapable of living a schedule.

3. *The examination of conscience*. It is impossible to attain personal excellence without frequent, preferably daily, resort to the examination of conscience. We should take three minutes towards the end of each day to review our behavior during the previous twenty-four hours. We should reflect on our failings and set concrete goals for the next day. In addition to this daily exam, it is a good idea to review several times a year in a more profound way how we have fared in living the leadership virtues.

And for those who really want to get down to brass tacks (a worthy ambition!), here are some detailed points on the two virtues specific to leadership—magnanimity and humility—and the four basic virtues—prudence, courage, self-control, and justice.

I urge you to take these points to your examination of conscience (and, indeed, to your prayer) as they indicate exactly where you need to be as a leader. You will see clearly where you are getting it right and where you need to improve.

If resorted to with regularity, these points will deepen your awareness that your professional excellence is not a matter of vainglory but a matter of God's will. If you take nothing else away from this book, let it be the conscientious and regular resort to these points aimed at helping you achieve personal excellence and effectiveness.

Magnanimity

☑ Am I aware of my dignity as a human being, and of the power of my mind, heart, and will? Am I aware of my personal freedom?

☑ I have been called to do great things, above all, to develop my personality and the personalities of those around me. Do I know this?

☑ Do I seek the company of magnanimous people, who, through their advice and by their example, help me to be magnanimous?

☑ Do I set high goals for myself and others? Do I strive, daily, to improve my character and behavior?

☑ Do I know what I am good at doing? Have I ever asked my friends to help me discover what I am good at, and to improve?

☑ As important as it is to struggle against my defects, I should be more concerned to develop and augment my strengths. Am I?

☑ Do I have confidence in myself, and in my talents and abilities?

☑ Have I discerned a mission in life?

☑ Do I focus on accomplishing my mission, or do I become distracted by peripheral matters?

☑ Do I try to inspire a sense of mission in my friends and colleagues?

☑ Do I give free rein to my imagination? Do I find ways to nourish it so that it bears more fruit?

☑ Am I able to make bold decisions or am I risk-averse? Does my fear of making mistakes cause me to be indecisive?

☑ The only thing I have to fear is not the evil that others do, but the good I fail to do. Do I realize this?

☑ Do I see obstacles as summits to be conquered, or do I give in to pessimism?

☑ Do I seek to address the problems of humanity? Do I see them as opportunities to grow in magnanimity?

Humility

☑ Do I respect the dignity of others, especially the ones I lead? Do I lead by example rather than compulsion, do I teach rather than command, inspire rather than browbeat? Leadership is less about displays of power than about the empowerment of others. Am I aware of this and do I act accordingly?

☑ Do I solicit the input of others in solving problems? Do I make use of their contributions?

- ☑ Do I refrain from interfering in the work of my subordinates, unless I have good reason? Do I avoid treating them like children?

- ☑ Do I avoid the temptation to do subordinates' work for them?

- ☑ Do I readily delegate power, i.e., transfer decision-making power, to subordinates?

- ☑ Do I foster in my team a culture of freedom and personal responsibility so that everyone truly participates in decision-making and feels accountable?

- ☑ Do I do everything I can to strengthen the commitment of team members to the shared mission?

- ☑ Do I draw out the reticent, encourage the domineering to yield, and help pessimists to see the positive side? Do I urge them to question conventional wisdom?

- ☑ Do I renounce my judgments (unless principles are at stake) when the group decides against my position? If, subsequently, a decision made against my advice proves mistaken, do I avoid saying, "I told you so"? Do I participate enthusiastically in the implementation of all decisions—even those I initially opposed?

- ☑ Do I promote my organization rather than myself? Do I avoid making myself indispensable? Do I share information? Do I create the conditions whereby others can successfully finish what I started?

☑ Do I choose my collaborators well, and pave the way for my succession? Do I find, develop, and encourage new leaders?

☑ Do I take pleasure in being of service? Do I cultivate altruistic motives?

☑ The employee who is motivated by a desire to serve is better suited for a leadership position than one more concerned to seek material rewards, no matter how brilliant his professional background. Am I aware of this?

☑ Am I concerned that those who work for and with me are happy? Do I take a proper interest in their professional success and financial security? Am I prepared to do what I can to help them achieve happiness in their personal and spiritual lives? Am I loyal to them?

☑ Do I learn from those I lead?

Prudence

☑ Before making a decision, do I analyze information critically? Do I assess the reliability of sources? Do I distinguish between facts and opinions, truths and half-truths?

☑ Instead of making decisions that correspond to the facts, do I bend the facts to serve my own interests? Do I reject truths I find hard to accept? This refusal to confront reality reflects a lack of courage on my part and renders the practice of prudence impossible. Am I aware of this?

- ☑ Am I humble enough to recognize and put aside my prejudices?

- ☑ Am I prone to accept as true whatever flatters my pride, or whatever satisfies my desire for money, fame, and pleasure? Virtues enable me to be objective, to perceive the world, human relationships and people as they really are, not as I wish them to be. Am I aware of this and do I seek to cultivate the virtues?

- ☑ Am I humble enough to learn from the experience of others?

- ☑ Am I convinced that management's top priority must be the accomplishment of the organization's mission? Does this mission determine and give meaning to objectives, or the other way around?

- ☑ Do I apply moral principles to achieve just outcomes? Do I realize there are many daunting moral and ethical challenges whose solutions are rarely to be found in textbooks?

- ☑ Do I seek advice? Do I choose associates who can challenge me?

- ☑ Do I take personal responsibility for my decisions? If things go wrong, do I refrain from blaming others?

- ☑ Do I fear making mistakes? Do I strive to overcome my fear? Am I aware that there is no such thing as scientific decision-making? The desire for absolute certainty is imprudent because it tends to paralyze one's ability to decide and act. Am I aware of this?

☑ Do I direct the carrying out of decisions expeditiously and with authority? Do I follow through on my decisions no matter how hard the going may get?

Courage

☑ Courage begins when I allow my conscience to be formed through a sincere and systematic search for truth. Am I aware of this?

☑ Is it clear what ideals I stand for? Is my behavior consistent? Do I worry about what others may say or think about me?

☑ Do I maintain the integrity of my conscience—even if I have to pay a price? Do I compromise my principles, justifying it by pointing to the amorality of others?

☑ Do I stay the course and maintain my focus? Do I persist despite obstacles? Do I bring my work to a proper conclusion, taking care to get the details right?

☑ Am I intelligent and principled in sticking to my views—or merely stubborn?

☑ Do I act boldly? Do I take prudent risks? Do I encourage risk-taking?

☑ Do I strive to overcome my fear of confrontation? Do I summon the courage to deal with difficult issues head-on? Do I have frank conversations with colleagues when necessary, or do I shy away from them?

☑ Do I defend the reputations of those who are the victims of malicious gossip or unfair criticism?

Self-control

☑ Self-control creates space in the heart for other people and for the ideal of serving them. Am I aware of this?

☑ Do I do what I *like* to do, or what I *should* be doing?

☑ Do I get caught up in doing what seems "urgent," rather than what is truly important? Do I devote sufficient time to what matters most—my personal development, the development of others, the professional and moral education of staff, long-term planning?

☑ Do I remain at peace even in trying circumstances? Do I respond calmly and courteously to criticism and opposition, never raising my voice or using vulgar language?

☑ Have I become a slave to money, power, fame and/or pleasure?

☑ Detachment from earthly things and purity of heart, mind and body are the wings that cause us to soar to the heights. Am I aware of this? Do I cultivate detachment?

Justice

☑ The faithful fulfillment of my professional, familial, and social responsibilities is an act of justice. Am I aware of this? Do I act accordingly? Do I strive for excellence in my work? Do I conceive of work as service to all?

☑ Am I devoted to family life? Am I aware of the difference between love for work and "workaholism"? Do I see family life as a source of strength? Do I realize that affection, trust, and openness are vital to personal happiness and professional effectiveness?

☑ Am I truthful, or is there a dichotomy between my interior self, and the face I show to the world? Do I strive to put an end to this contradiction? Am I determined to put aside all phoniness?

☑ Do I stand for moral truth, even if this means contradicting political correctness and provoking opposition?

☑ Do I see colleagues and employees as objects to be manipulated—or as persons to be served?

☑ Am I aware that people are persons and not abstract factors of production? Do I realize that it is impossible for me to give them their due, as justice demands, if I do not love them?

☑ Do I cultivate friendships—or mere relationships? Am I aware that friendship is another name for service?

◇   ◇   ◇

POSTSCRIPT 2—Response to Critics

In this postscript I would like to answer some of the criticisms that have been made of my first book *Virtuous Leadership*.

I have been criticized for having founded my system of leadership on a moral concept comprehensible only to Europeans.

In fact, there is no moral concept more universal than virtue. The moral tradition of the Far East is based on the same intuitions as Aristotelian ethics.[2] It is virtue that makes a man a man ("ren" in Chinese, "jin" in Japanese). The man without virtue (fei-ren, hi-nin) is the "non-man" as indicated by the ideogram below, which represents negation and the lie (interior

---

2. Cf. Jiyuan Yu, *The Ethics of Confucius and Aristotle: Mirrors of Virtue* (New York: Routledge), 2007.

disintegration) juxtaposed with the ideogram representing man:

非人

I was not surprised when less than a year after the publication of the English original I heard that Chinese people had already translated several chapters of *Virtuous Leadership*.

It is not ancient but modern philosophy—starting with René Descartes and culminating in Emmanuel Kant—that is hard for non-Europeans to comprehend.

I have been criticized for rejecting the traditional schema whereby magnanimity is considered a part of the virtue of courage, and humility a part of the virtue of self-control.

I am not the first one to have done so. Many commentators have noted the artificiality of making magnanimity a part of courage[3] and the arbitrariness of making humility a part of self-control.[4] These

---

3. "If Thomas Aquinas did not break the link binding magnanimity and courage, he made it as tenuous as possible. In the *Summa Theologica* II. II. 140, 2 ad 1, he gives us to understand that linking magnanimity to courage is artificial," affirms R. A. Gauthier, one of the greatest Thomists of the twentieth century (See R. A. Gauthier, *Magnanimité*, 363).

4. "Certainly, Thomas Aquinas links humility to self-control. But one must not be deceived by this classification, which is to a great extent arbitrary," affirms R. A. Gauthier in the spirit of R. P. Sertillanges, another Thomist of international reputation (R. A. Gauthier, *Magnanimité*, 460; R. P. Sertillanges, *La Philosophie morale de Saint Thomas d'Aquin* [Paris: Nouvelle Edition, 1941], 353).

linkages are not to be found in Aristotle,[5] and although not devoid of logic, they are of no practical value or interest.[6]

I have been criticized for not having mentioned prudence (practical wisdom) as a virtue specific to leadership. But prudence, although *fundamental* to leadership (like courage, self-control, and justice), is not *specific* to leadership. Without prudence, leadership fails, but it is not prudence that creates leadership.

Prudence is the specific virtue of decision-makers. But a person who makes good decisions is not necessarily a good leader. He will only be a good leader if he possesses magnanimity and humility. Decisions proper to leaders—decisions that bring out the greatness in people—are magnanimous and humble decisions, and not decisions that are merely prudent.

I was criticized for having mentioned Jesus Christ and Christianity in a book on leadership and personal excellence.

Truth to tell, if I had not spoken of Christ and Christianity, I would have been guilty of intellectual dishonesty, ingratitude, and impiety.

Of intellectual dishonesty because Jesus Christ is the perfect model of leadership, the perfect model of

---

5. These ideas are found in the Stoic philosophy of Chrysippus (280–206 BC), who made the virtue of magnanimity a part of courage, and in a treatise entitled *De passionibus*, falsely attributed to Andronicus of Rhodes (first century BC), that makes humility a part of the virtue of self-control for the first time.

6. Cf. R. A. Gauthier. *Magnanimité*, 363.

magnanimity and humility; of ingratitude because without the input of Christian philosophy and theology I
would have been incapable of writing *Virtuous Leadership* in the first place; of impiety because my "method"
would have turned out to be a diabolical trick.

Impiety—that was the thing I most wanted to
avoid. When I felt the temptation to exclude Christ
and Christianity, I remembered the book by Vladimir
Soloviev, the Russian philosopher and visionary, called
A Short Tale of the Antichrist. Written several months
before his death in 1900, it speaks of a "remarkable
man" who will appear at the beginning of the twenty-
first century in the "United States of Europe" and will
set forth a plan for universal peace and prosperity that
"pleases everyone," conferring on him vast power and
celebrity. This plan is based on Christian values, and
yet "does not mention the name of Christ at all." The
"remarkable man" is, of course, the Antichrist. That I
would write a book largely inspired by Christian ideals, and yet not mention Christ, would mean I was in
the same league as Soloviev's Antichrist. This thought
caused me considerable malaise.

After 2,000 years of Christianity, to speak of man,
his greatness, his vocation to perfection without men-
tioning Christ would be to take a position *against*
Christ—either out of conviction, like the Pharisees, or
out of fear, like the mobs that demanded his crucifixion.

I have been criticized for a number of things. This
has not surprised me. *Virtuous Leadership* is not a traditional book. Inevitably, it has shocked those who

cannot or will not change their rigid ways of thinking. What *has* surprised me is the enthusiasm the book has evoked around the world, including in Western Europe, where anti-Christian prejudice remains very strong. Between 2007 and 2011, *Virtuous Leadership* has been translated into fifteen languages.